The

Language

They Speak

Is Things

to Eat

The

University

of North

Carolina

Press

Chapel Hill

& London

Betty Adcock

A. R. Ammons

Maya Angelou

James Applewhite

Gerald Barrax

Kathryn Stripling Byer

Fred Chappell

William Harmon

Susan Ludvigson

Michael McFee

Heather Ross Miller

Robert Morgan

Reynolds Price

James Seay

Jonathan Williams

The Language They Speak

Poems
by
Fifteen
Contemporary
North
Carolina
Poets

. . . .

Is Things
to Eat

Edited
by
Michael
McFee

Library of Congress

Cataloging-in-Publication Data

The Language they speak is things to eat : poems by fifteen

contemporary North Carolina poets / edited by Michael

McFee.

   p. cm.

ISBN 0-8078-2172-1 (cloth : alk. paper). —

ISBN 0-8078-4483-7 (pbk. : alk. paper)

   1. American poetry—North Carolina. 2. American

poetry—20th century. 3. North Carolina—Poetry.

I. McFee, Michael.

PS558.N8L36   1994

813'.540809756—dc20   94-4239

                                                        CIP

98   97   96   95   94   5   4   3   2   1

For my son

PHILIP

and all future

generations of

North Carolina

writers and

readers

Contents

. . . .

Acknowledgments

. . . .

Thanks to the poets of North Carolina, for writing such fine poems and allowing me to make the present selection. May this book help bring them some of the audience they deserve.

Thanks to their presses, for granting permission to reprint their poems, as itemized in the permissions section at the end of the book. May this anthology encourage readers to seek out and buy the poets' individual volumes.

Thanks to the Committee on Faculty Research and Study Leaves at the University of North Carolina at Chapel Hill, for a 1994 Junior Faculty Development Award that greatly helped with expenses incurred during this project.

Thanks to Anne Weston, for stepping forward and helping with the text at a crucial stage. I appreciate her cheerful, able, and very punctual assistance.

And thanks to the folks at the University of North Carolina Press, especially David Perry, Barbara Hanrahan, and Sarah Nawrocki. As a writer and reader and native North Carolinian, I appreciate their commitment to the excellent contemporary literature of our state.

Introduction

Several decades ago, spelunking through a library's dim stacks, scanning the poetry shelves for something interesting, I pulled down a book called *Red Owl* by a poet named Robert Morgan. Neither was familiar to me. But as I began reading those brief, vivid poems, suddenly they seemed *very* familiar to me: because this poet was writing about something I knew, the landscape and the people and the things of the North Carolina mountains, my home.

I was exhilarated. I had never considered the remote Blue Ridge as a valid subject for poetry: Morgan introduced me to a whole new range of possibilities, as a reader and as a young writer. And the more I read in *Red Owl*—and in other books of poems by other North Carolinians, like Fred Chappell and Jonathan Williams, A. R. Ammons and James Applewhite—the more intrigued I became. There seemed to be a body of poetry native to our state that was not mere local color versifying, that had the virtues of the best poetry anywhere: fresh imagination, verbal intensity, formal variety and accomplishment, and above all a sense of humor and humanness that made the poems a pleasure to read.

As luck would have it, I started reading contemporary North Carolina poets at just the right time. Since the mid-1970s, there has been a steadily increasing harvest of first-rate books by these writers, one that has only deepened my initial enthusiasm. This anthology is the first attempt of its kind to sample that delightful bounty.

Anthologies are, by their very nature, selective: they are bouquets rather than whole fields of flowers. But though the principles of selection may vary, most anthologists seem to favor variety over depth, offering—by way of introduction or overview—as many poets as possible, with a few poems each. And most anthologies of North Carolina poetry have followed this pattern, beginning with Mary Bayard Clarke's *Wood-Notes; or, Carolina Carols* in 1854, with its opening fanfare: "Come rouse you! ye poets of North Carolina, / My State is my theme and I seek not a finer." Subsequent anthologies—in 1877, 1912, 1941, 1951, 1963, 1977, and 1982—have also, by inclination or necessity, taken the quantitative approach. For example, the most recent full-scale collection, Guy Owen and Mary Williams's *Contemporary Poetry of North Carolina* (1977), presented sixty-three poets, with one to four poems each.

This is a different manner of anthology. Rather than offering quick tastes of many poets, then snatching readers off to another dish in the poetry buffet once they've found something they like, this anthology offers generous servings of fewer poets. Such a presentation, I hope, gives a more accurate and satisfying sense of a poet's full flavor. Just as fiction writers may need ten or fifteen pages in order to fully develop a story, poets benefit from a more substantial sampling of their work, something more comprehensive than a single lyric poem, however delicious.

Poems can be characterized by what they leave out as well as what they include. So can anthologies like *The Language They Speak Is Things to Eat*.

This book does not include such distinguished deceased North Carolina poets as Carl Sandburg, Randall Jarrell, and O. B. Hardison, Jr. Neither does it include those veteran North Carolina poets whose presence on the state's poetry scene since the early 1960s has been invaluable, people like Robert Watson, Ann Deagon, Ronald Bayes, and Sam Ragan. Nor does it include some fine North Carolina poets—like Shirley Anders, Michael Chitwood, or Deborah Pope—who have published only a single full-length volume.

Who *is* included, then? This anthology gathers fifteen living poets whose chief creative work has been done in the last twenty years, between 1973 and 1993, with a focus on the past decade. Their poetry must have been published in at least two full-length books during that time. This is a selection of the lyric poems deemed worthy (by authors and their publishers) to appear in individual volumes; it excerpts no long poems and reprints no uncollected work or poems published solely in limited editions, chapbooks, or magazines.

And, finally, the poet must be a North Carolina poet.

Just what is a "North Carolina poet"? A poet, first of all: one who writes poems, has done so for a long time, and (Emily Dickinson notwithstanding) has published the work in books, with some measure of success or attention. The poets in this book have an exemplary record of publications, readings, positions, and awards: they have won Bollingen Prizes, several Lamont Prizes, and numerous distinguished fellowships. And—as with the contemporary North Carolina fiction writers in *The Rough Road Home* (University of North Carolina Press, 1992)—the work itself is first-rate, worthy of inclusion in any representative anthology of contemporary writing, whatever the parameters.

But what makes these fifteen poets distinctively *North Carolina* poets? That's a tough question, a more localized version of the "What is a Southern writer?" conundrum. I won't reprise all the weary answers to that worn-out regional question, all the thematic or stylistic or cultural concerns that cause us to group writers by nation or region or state or city. Instead, I'll offer—by way of conclusion—my own equivocal answer:

They are North Carolina poets because they choose to be so.

By which I mean this. All of these poets—whether they were born here and stayed, or born here and left, or born here and left and returned, or moved here and stayed—have made North Carolina a matter of choice, of allegiance. They have "identified themselves as North Carolinians," as Richard Walser phrased it in his preface to *North Carolina Poetry* (1941). Those who are still living here could probably be living somewhere else, professionally speaking, but they aren't; and those who are living elsewhere could certainly choose not to return home in their poems, but they frequently do. There's something about this place that attracts their attention, their eye and ear and tongue, their heart and mind, their appetite; and if the nature of that attraction is complex or paradoxical—well, so is a good poem. There's something about the landscape, and the history, and the people, and the language, and the food, and the weather, and the very air of this place that permeates the verbal consciousness of a North Carolina poet. In fact, it's as if—by birth or longtime residence—North Carolina has chosen *them*, and they are working out that odd bond in concentrated lines and words, in the distilled spirits of poetry.

Every anthology should begin with an apology: though such a gathering should be useful and delightful, it is still a distortion of the available body of literature, one editor's funny-mirror compression of what (especially in the case of poetry) has already been compressed to the verbal essentials.

My apologies to the poets whom—due to space considerations—I could not include. Given the vigorous and intimate poetry community in North Carolina, this was particularly painful to me.

My apologies to the poets I did include, for having to cut—again, due to space limitations—poems that surely deserve to be here.

But, mostly, I feel less apologetic than hugely grateful—for the luck of having been born here, at this literary time; for the delight of discovering these poets long ago; for the pleasure of reading their work as it appeared and developed; for the satisfaction of re-reading it as I assembled this book; and for the privilege of putting this book together.

The poets are presented here alphabetically. Their poems are arranged chronologically, by date of book publication—progressing from the earliest to the most recent—with an occasional shift for the sake of pacing or juxtaposition. Following the main text are brief essays about the poets, with critical commentary and biographical information, as well as selected bibliographies.

The title of this anthology, *The Language They Speak Is Things to Eat*, is a line from James Applewhite's poem "Some Words for Fall." It refers to tobacco workers in eastern North Carolina, whose speech is no less appetizing than barbecue, no less succulent and satisfying. As I hope the following poems show, the same is true of the North Carolina poets in this anthology. The words they say are not self-consciously difficult or private or obscure, as contemporary poetry is often accused of being: rather, their poems are direct and engaging, rich in image and character and story and humor, with a genuine love of place. For any reader, the language they speak is truly things to eat.

· · · · · · · ·

BETTY ADCOCK

Southbound

You can go back in a clap of blue metal
tracked by stewardesses with drinks and virginal masks.
These will work whether you breathe or not. And this
is the first part. The way is farther
into thin roads that sway with the country.
Through the shine of a rented car the red towns rise
and crumble, leaving faces stuck to you like dust.
Following the farms, houses the color of old women,
you gather a cargo from yards full of lapsed
appliances, tin cans, crockery, snapped wheels,
weedy, bottomless chairs. These float through the air
to rest on the sleek hood, the clean seats.
Things broken out of their forms
move to you, their owner, their own.
You slow under weight. The windshield blurs
with the wingbeat of chickens. The hound's
voice takes over your horn.
A green glass vase from a grave in a field
comes flowerless to your hand, holds a smell
of struck matches, of summer on rust, of running
water, of rabbits, of home.

Then the one place flung up like a barrier,
the place where you stop, the last
courthouse and gathering of garrulous stores.
You have brought the town.
It walks in your skin like a visitor.
Here, under the wooden tongue of the church,
by the paths with their toothed gates,
in the light of the drunk as he burns
past hunkered children reaching
for the eyes of their fathers, these fading
and coming like seasons,
you are the tall rooms of your dead.

Merchants still ring small furious bells
and the window of the moviehouse opens,
and the girls who will, open.
Men still stand jack-knifed to trace
deer trails in the dirt.
And blacks scythe the lawns, not singing,
keeping their flag hidden.

You may house again these weathers worn thin
as coins that won't spend, worn smooth
as the years between two who are old
and not fooled any longer. You may stand
beneath the cafe's blue sign where it steps
on the face like a fly. You may bend
to finger the cracked sidewalk,
the shape of stilled lightning, every fork
the same as it was when you thought that map
led to the rim of the world.

You may listen for thunder.

·   ·   ·   ·   ·   ·   ·

Walking Out

Fishing alone in a frail boat
he leaned too far, lost hold,
was turned out of the caulked world.
Seventy years he had lived without learning
how surfaces keep the swimmer up.

In that green fall, the churn of fear
slowing to pavane,
one breath held precious and broken,
he counted oar-strokes backward:
shore was not far.
This coin he took from the pocket of terror.

Starting over, over his head,
he reached for the earth.
As creatures of water once called on the future
locked in their bodies, he called on his past.
He walked. Walked. And there was enough
time, just enough, and luck.
Touching greenfingered sand, rising and touching,
body bursting with useless knowledge,
he came at the world from its other direction
and came to his place in air.

Back in his life now, he measures
distances one breath long,
talks less, flexes
the oars of his legs.

Things shimmer where he is,
his house, his earthcolored wife and sons.
Every place raises walls around him
the color of old glass.
Heaven is a high clear skin.

Beneath the drift of flesh his bones remember
trying for bottom.

· · · · · · ·

Hand Made

It squats like a shipwreck
or a child's just-outsized coffin lifted up
by floodwaters into wrong light,
the quilt chest—my great-grandmother's hold
on what they were and wore in their keeping
from true cold,
in their rolling each morning from under
the pieced, turned-over fields of their lives.
It's too heavy for any room of mine.

The wide lid is one board,
heart of a pine we'd never recognize,
shut now upon nearly nothing,
a faint salt dust only,
flakings from the dreamed-under patterns,
leather-flecks from saved baby shoes,
sweet odor of dead sex, vinegar of sweat,
breath caught
a hundred and fifty years
in this wood's strong current.

Those missing
from photographs, gene-strands, thumbprints,
tinkering spirits,
threads from the absent restless
bedclothes—a leakage unwanted as the light
old fear and love let into hard sleep,
sap from the original
tree it is my own voice saying

green and yellow, whole skies, blue
herons, lilies, rings, glassware, cows,
orchards, pistols, red hats, mayhaws,
the heart's loose change flying.

If you say you would go to that country,
here is the boat and the river.
So the way is pure mourning. So we'll weep!
We'll know everything, weeping for so many,
hearing the huge, deep-starred tree
as it answers us, needle after needle,
with these thick, muddy colors for weather,
these sharp little stitches holding on
across the eyes,
under the breastbone.

One Street

No one speaks of the way
towns shrink in the night,
the world taking them back
bit by little bit.
They give in
the way faces do underground.

Days, our mirage keeps things going.
Only the old people know,
dozing at noon,
how the porch rails soften
and the stairs give up their nails,
the roof sifting down, down
the little speeches of dust.
Only the old people know this,
asleep at all hours,
their breath our shelter.

. . . .

Front Porch

for Del Marie Rogers

This is deep-roofed shelter
for a roomful of weather,
the first and last of the journey,

and a boundary you can stand on
from inside or outside
without taking a position.

Anything can meet anything
where household touches wider
world in mud-tracks on the floor.

Here, rocking chairs turn back
on what is left of winter,
bent mourners against the housewall.

We've mostly given it up for lost,
made do with a backyard deck at most.
The cost of that is in direction.

But even now, sometimes, you'll hear one
called home,
that sound like nothing but wind

plucking a long wooden swing
whose arms are full of leaves and lamplight,
shadow-trees on the tall steps, climbing.

.   .   .   .

Roller Rink

That summer it just appeared,
like a huge canvas butterfly
pinned to McNaughton's field.
All of us half-grown came every day
to watch and try, in love
with unlikely motion, with ourselves
and the obscure brother
who was older and came from a nameless far end
of the county. He knew, from somewhere,
how to do it, the dance of it turning
faster than music, could bend
and glide smooth as a fish where we fell,
could leap, land and roll on
squatting, backward, one-footed.
We loved him for looking blade-boned and frail,
for being always alone with nothing to tell.

In August the old man who'd taken our change
hefted sections of floor and his tent
and his music into a truckbed and left.
The autumn that came after
rose for us with so perfectly clear
a cry of wild geese and amber light
on its early winds, with so many stars
let loose, and leaves in the rain—
even our shambling, hopeless town
seemed good, just in that turn
before the wheel of the year came down.

Of course it never came again.
There was the round brown place
where grass wouldn't grow in that field,
but would grow next year with great ghost wheels
of Queen Anne's lace.
That summer was a line we'd stumbled over,
and so we were free to fall and gather
the dear, unskillful, amazing losses
departure needs. We took them all,
our bodies shooting crazily
into and through each other. And finally past
to army, city, anyplace far.
We took any road out we could take;
but none of us with the sweet-lifting grace
and ease of the promise that farm boy made
who went and stayed.

. . . .

Poetry Workshop in a
Maximum Security Reform School

I brought them an armful of apples,
incense, and a branch of autumn leaves.
These children have eaten the incense.

Green dye in the stuff has printed their mouths
and is harmless, though they hate and hope.
They have rolled up the leaves for smoking
and have opened the apples, joking of razorblades.

Greenfaced and sick of the artful
part-time in their time that is whole,
they know any word is the same knife
and that blood is so simple
it only wants to get out.
I say I understand. I do. So I start again
on the scarred blackboard:

    poem   *weapon*

. . . .

Clearing Out, 1974

After this kind of death, sudden and violent,
there's difference forever in the light.
Here's the sun I'll see from now on
aslant and keeping nothing
in its backward look. I have become rich
with disappearance. I have become this light

pooled now on my father's desk,
his grandfather's—rolltop sturdy as a boat
and ice-locked in a century of deepening afternoon.
I have to open it and take the cargo on
myself. There's no one else.

Forget the pigeonholes with their indifferently kept
papers waiting to fly out and be important.
They were never important, the cash and receipts,
leases, royalties, mortgages wadded here like trash.
Forget the checkbook that was awash with blood,
and the wallet, its pictures crusted dark.
Everything in his pockets was afloat.

A man shot in the stomach drowns
what's on him. Let the *personal effects*
stay in their labeled plastic sack. Go on

as if this were a forest with a path.
It's like him to have kept a jay's flightfeather,
old now to crumbling, though it holds to blue
like a blind man's memory of sky;
and a terrapin shell bleached of all camouflage,
white dome of cyclopean masonry in scale,
packed with the shape of silence as a bell;
a wild boar's intact lower jaw, the yellowed tusks
like twists of evil weather caught in sculpture,
dusty in a scatter of red cartouches,
the shotgun cartridges gone soft as cloth.

One drawer's half filled with pocketknives,
all sizes, jumble of dark hafts like a cache
of dried fish. Opened, these could still
swim through to sapling heart. To bone.

He had a good eye. With any kind of blade
he'd make a creature walk straight out of wood
into your hand. The few he didn't give away
are gathered here, votive and reliquary:

bear with her hitch-legged cub,
dove in a tree, wild turkey open-winged,
two deer with antlers slightly off
—imperfect the way antlers really are—
and a razorback, a bobcat in a leap.
And then the horses.
My mother gave him real woodcarver's knives,
cherished in their box and not once used.

The best of the figures is the bucking horse,
body like a hauled-back bow.
Even on this scale the strain, the shine

of muscle showing, wind in a flung stirrup.
And all the intricate heave of wished-for power
is drawn down to a block two inches square,
four hooves and the head locked on the moment
arching off that little ground.

Drawerful of keys, marbles, arrowheads, rocks
he saw some form in. Keys to nothing standing.
There's a grace to the thin-shanked instruments
whose ends look like dull claws, the kind old houses
had for every room; blunter keys for barn lots,
cabins that held the violated lives of slaves,
cotton houses, lawyers' offices, stores
that ran on barter.

A peace comes to this sorting.
When my grandmother was a girl, she raised a fawn.
It went wild afterward in our woods. Later,
a buck full-grown thumped up the steps one night
onto the porch outside this very window,
slipping and knocking antlers on the rail.
Framed in the lamplight for one still moment,
the strange known eyes looked in,
and the young woman looked out at him.
It's the part of every story we remember,

the dream lost track of, changed
and coming back.

Distance has webbed my eyes like cataract,
thickening like an ice sheet I must lift.
Heavy with damp,
here is the Teal Bible, 1815,
brought to Texas with the first encampment
of Anglo settlers. It's pure living mystery
why they came. Unless that's what they came for
after all, with no way to answer
except the ways to kill; and no new dream enough

to staunch the stubborn longing to recover
what vanished in their footprints.

My great-grandfather's whistle carved of horn.

A cedar knot, deep turn in the red heart
heavy and separate. Nick it, and the scent
of cedar pours out like a sound, that thick.

Wild turkey caller whittled out of pine,
all confirmation gone.

The hunter's horn with one note for the lost.

And a perfect doll-sized real cane-bottomed
chair in a bottle.

That's the lot. I'll take what matters,
blood and documents, to the life I made elsewhere,
that place so far different in this light
you could get the bends between here and there.
The animals in wood, the stones, the silence caught
in terrapin's shell and turkey's pine voicebox,
this desk itself—a beholding full
of time before the tree was cut to build it—
I set all adrift, dismantled vessel, log raft,
rough-layered rings of association
like a language widening.
And the loosed river takes it
toward the turning sawblades of our dawn.

A Greek poet said it. Thémelis:
What would death have been without us?

Remembering Brushing My Grandmother's Hair

I see her in a ring of sewing, light
fingers on needle and hoop, elaborate
scissors shaped like a tiny stork,
the glass egg in her lap.
Her temperate mourning wore black shoes.

Released, her hair released a scent
as I imagined of ascending birds, or smoke
from a burning without source, but cool
as mist over a real country, altars in the hills.
That gray reached all the way to the floor.

A cloak, wind in a cloak, her hair
in my hands crackled and flew. I dreamed her
young and flying from some tallest room
before she had to let her power down
for something to take hold and climb.

Permanence. Rose and vine were twisted
hard in silver on the brush and mirror.
Above us, the accurate clock pinged:
always on a time there comes a sleep
stony as a tower, with the wild world beneath,

and wound like this with locked bloom tarnishing—
I brushed. She sewed or dozed. The child I was
stood shoulder-deep in dying, in a dress of falling
silver smoothed by silver, a forgetfulness
dimming the trees outside the window like a rain.

To grow to stay, to braid and bend
from one high window—
I guessed the story I would learn by heart:
how women's hands among sharp instruments
learn sleep, the frieze like metal darkening,
the land sown deep with salt.

Exchange

In the cavernous, tin-ceilinged back room
of THE FARMER'S EXCHANGE, GENERAL MERCHANDISE,
cloth sacks of flour were piled in a mountain
shedding constant snow, powdering a weave of its own
on the stacked extra harnesses, bullwhips, boxes
of boots, nail barrels, dead cockroaches,
and the flypaper hanging in useless loops.

Saturdays we sneaked there to ruin
all credible arrangement, to burn up
in a white summer of dreams while the working
sun edged in the back door from the alley,
slow as another customer with no money.

Hefting walls of our future bread
into castles and forts, we leaped over
to land in original tracks, explorers.
We knew the movies, a few books, school-yard sex—
everything in the world that we knew
was usable. Once I dropped a lit cigarette
between slats of a crate, and we couldn't get to it.
All that night in our beds awake,
we kept a pact of prayer against fire,
against sirens that could unzip the dark,
everything that we knew in the world
its flammable secret.

We wrote notes in code, left them rolled
in the empty throats of pop bottles
crated to go, addressed to kindred souls
surely trapped at the far end of Coca-Cola's line,
forced there to wash and refill maybe a million,
and waiting for rescue only we could arrange.
Whatever was beyond changing waited for us.

Through the arch between storeroom and trade,
we could just see our mothers and fathers
still talking up front. And they paled
in the white breath made of our motion.
We could let them go on fading forever
in the storm we had hung on the air.
Or we could come forth and forgive them
back to the living.

Found, dragged home to be scolded,
we left our ghost step on the sidewalk.
Probably somebody would have to pay
for a bag of flour broken,
and always we would have to say we were sorry
and be looked at, bad children
bleached as biscuits, encoded as spirits,
shaking our real hair out of a cloud.

Were we not beautiful then?—miller's daughters
able to spin and be counted, warriors,
discoverers willing to get there in time,
ourselves the gold coming through.

. . . .

Rent House

I can't think why I've come to see this
house with no resonance, temporary
years between the real houses: that one
I was born to, the other I traveled from.
The interim is here, habitual, stupefied
summers of brass and blue enamel,
smudged backyard grass of fall.
Everything that was here still
stands except the cannas. The journey
of the same cracked two-strip driveway
ends the same.

Before this, the short life it feels like dreaming
to remember: field and barn, pecan trees,
the rambling gentle house holding its own
wide skirts of pasture, fluttering henyard,
and my live mother close.
The town doctor's had that place for thirty years,
all the pecans, sunset behind the fence rail,
a bed of asters in the filled-in fish pool.

The last of childhood left me in yet another
house, five unsteady porches, grandparents,
a spread wing floating me along until I simmered
into leaving.
Years ago, a retired contractor from Houston
restored that one to unremembered splendor.

This narrow house between.
I look a long time, thinking
I need imagination, but there's nothing
to be made of such temporal defeat.
How long was it we lived on this back street
behind screens billowing with rust?
I remember how long one afternoon
I wrote my whole name broad and hard in crayon
on every single windowscreen in this house,
and then was punished.
Forsythia is the name of those flowers
I watched darken in the wallpaper.

All night I'd listen to the child next door
cry and cut teeth. Now he's a lawyer
in San Francisco. I matched his howls
with those I kept back. Both our voices
ran down the moony street alongside crossed
adult allegiances that roamed, like ghostly wolves,
the nights of any town so old.

Nobody rented in a town like this.
Why did papa bring me here
to this aunt who makes me braid my hair?
Where is my mother?
Where's the calf you said was mine?
What happened to the trees?
Then they'd drive me out there so I'd see
fields dizzy with briers, the derelict house
large and sad and creatureless.
Until I lost even my loss, got used
to a cramped hallway and a makeshift life,
the tight backyard with no hen in it.

And it was here I staked a claim: from any room
I could look up to see my name
purple or lime green against the sun,
or clearer, lamplit on the night outside.
Nothing they tried would get it off
those years I thinned down, toughening,
asthmatic with grief and discovery:
how the self, amazed, swam up like bone
through the lost landscape, through the mother's
vanished flesh, through all remembered
and all future home,
to build garish letters on the riddled air,
knowing there's no place else. Not anywhere.

. . . .

A. R. AMMONS

Uppermost

The top
grain on the peak
weighs next
to nothing and,
sustained
by a mountain,
has no burden,
but nearly
ready to float,
exposed
to summit wind,
it endures
the rigors of having
no further
figure to complete
and a
blank sky
to guide its dreaming

.   .   .   .

Double Exposure

Flounder-like, poetry
flattens white
against bottom mud

so farthest tremors can get
full-ranged to the bone:
but on the side it flowers

invisible with blue mud-work
imitations, it
turns both eyes.

Strolls

The brook gives me
sparkles plenty, an
abundance, but asks
nothing of me:
snow thickets
and scrawny
snowwork of hedgerows,
still gold weeds, and
snow-bent cedar gatherings
provide
feasts of disposition
(figure, color, weight, proportion)
and require
not even that I notice:
the near-winter quartermoon
sliding high almost
into color at four-thirty—
the abundance of clarity
along the rose ridge line!
alone, I'm not alone:
a standoffishness and reasonableness
in things finds
me or I find that
in them: sand, falls,
furrow, bluff—
things one, speaking things
not words, would
have found to say.

· · · · · · · ·

Ballad

I want to know the unity in all things and the difference
between one thing and another
    I said to the willow

and asked what it wanted to know: the willow said it
wanted to know how to get rid of the wateroak
that was throwing it into shade every afternoon at 4 o'clock:
    that is a real problem I said I suppose
and the willow, once started, went right on saying
I can't take you for a friend because while you must
be interested in willowness, which you could find nowhere
  better than right here,
    I'll bet you're just as interested in wateroakness
which you can find in a pure form right over there,
a pure form of evil and death to me:
I know I said I want to be friends with you both but the
willow sloughed into a deep grief
and said
if you could just tie back some of those oak branches
until I can get a little closer to mastering that domain
of space up there—see it? how empty it is
and how full of light:
    why I said don't I ask the wateroak if he would mind
withholding himself until you're more nearly even: after
all I said you are both trees and you both need water and
light and space to unfold into, surely the wateroak will
understand that commonness:
  not so you could tell it, said the willow:
    that I said is cynical and uncooperative: what could
you give the wateroak in return for his withholding:
what could I give him, said the willow, nothing
that he hasn't already taken:
  well, I said, but does he know about the unity in
all things, does he understand that all things have a
common source and end: if he could be made
to see that rather deeply, don't you think he might
    give you a little way:
no said the willow he'd be afraid I would take all:
would you I said:
or would you, should the need come, give him a little way
back:
    I would said the willow but my need is greater than

his
and the trade would not be fair:
maybe not I said but let's approach him with our powerful
concept that all things are in all
    and see if he will be moved

. . . .

Certainty

I have certainly felt the documentation of terror:
I have certainly known my
insides to turn all hands
and rush to the surface for help
and felt the hands go loose:
I certainly have come to believe in death;
my head rustles with footnotes and
quotation marks
that pinpoint places where my blood
has certainly stopped cold and certainly raced.

. . . .

80-Proof

A fifth of me's me:
the rest's chaser:
35 lbs.'s
my true self: but
chuck 10 lbs. or so for bones,
what's left's
steaks & chops &
chicken fat,
two-over-easy & cream-on-the-side:
strip off a sheath of hide,
strip out nerves & veins
& permeable membranes,
what's left's a greasy spot:

the question's
whether
to retain
the shallow stain
or go 100% spiritual
and fifth by fifth
achieve a whole,
highly transcendental.

. . . .

Rapids

Fall's leaves are redder than
spring's flowers, have no pollen,
and also sometimes fly, as the wind
schools them out or down in shoals
or droves: though I
have not been here long, I can
look up at the sky at night and tell
how things are likely to go for
the next hundred million years:
the universe will probably not find
a way to vanish nor I
in all that time reappear.

. . . .

Easter Morning

I have a life that did not become,
that turned aside and stopped,
astonished:
I hold it in me like a pregnancy or
as on my lap a child
not to grow or grow old but dwell on

it is to his grave I most
frequently return and return
to ask what is wrong, what was
wrong, to see it all by
the light of a different necessity
but the grave will not heal
and the child,
stirring, must share my grave
with me, an old man having
gotten by on what was left

when I go back to my home country in these
fresh far-away days, it's convenient to visit
everybody, aunts and uncles, those who used to say,
look how he's shooting up, and the
trinket aunts who always had a little
something in their pocketbooks, cinnamon bark
or a penny or nickel, and uncles who
were the rumored fathers of cousins
who whispered of them as of great, if
troubled, presences, and school
teachers, just about everybody older
(and some younger) collected in one place
waiting, particularly, but not for
me, mother and father there, too, and others
close, close as burrowing
under skin, all in the graveyard
assembled, done for, the world they
used to wield, have trouble and joy
in, gone

the child in me that could not become
was not ready for others to go,
to go on into change, blessings and
horrors, but stands there by the road
where the mishap occurred, crying out for
help, come and fix this or we
can't get by, but the great ones who

were to return, they could not or did
not hear and went on in a flurry and
now, I say in the graveyard, here
lies the flurry, now it can't come
back with help or helpful asides, now
we all buy the bitter
incompletions, pick up the knots of
horror, silently raving, and go on
crashing into empty ends not
completions, not rondures the fullness
has come into and spent itself from

I stand on the stump
of a child, whether myself
or my little brother who died, and
yell as far as I can, I cannot leave this place, for
for me it is the dearest and the worst,
it is life nearest to life which is
life lost: it is my place where
I must stand and fail,
calling attention with tears
to the branches not lofting
boughs into space, to the barren
air that holds the world that was my world

though the incompletions
(& completions) burn out
standing in the flash high-burn
momentary structure of ash, still it
is a picture-book, letter-perfect
Easter morning: I have been for a
walk: the wind is tranquil: the brook
works without flashing in an abundant
tranquility: the birds are lively with
voice: I saw something I had
never seen before: two great birds,
maybe eagles, blackwinged, whitenecked
and -headed, came from the south oaring

the great wings steadily; they went
directly over me, high up, and kept on
due north: but then one bird,
the one behind, veered a little to the
left and the other bird kept on seeming
not to notice for a minute: the first
began to circle as if looking for
something, coasting, resting its wings
on the down side of some of the circles:
the other bird came back and they both
circled, looking perhaps for a draft;
they turned a few more times, possibly
rising—at least, clearly resting—
then flew on falling into distance till
they broke across the local bush and
trees: it was a sight of bountiful
majesty and integrity: the having
patterns and routes, breaking
from them to explore other patterns or
better ways to routes, and then the
return: a dance sacred as the sap in
the trees, permanent in its descriptions
as the ripples round the brook's
ripplestone: fresh as this particular
flood of burn breaking across us now
from the sun.

· · · · · · · ·

Night Finding

Open and naked under the big snow
the hill cemetery by the falls
looks felled to stump stone

and the rich spray of the summer
falls gathers absent into
glazes of ice wall: here in the

backyard thicket sway-floats
of honeysucklebush brush
(once misted berry red)

bend down to solid touch,
and weed clumps break off
into halfway teepees:

pheasant in the earliest pearl
of dusk bluster in, swirls of
landing and looking, and settled

to the dusk mode, walk under
the snow slants and shelters easing
through brush fox would noticeably jar.

. . . .

Parting

She was already lean when
a stroke or two slapped
her face like drawn
claw prints: akilter, she
ate less and

sat too much on the edge
of beds looking a width too
wide out of windows:
she lessened: getting
out for a good day, she sat

on the bench still and
thin as a porch post:
the children are all
off, she would think, but a
minute later,

startle, where are the children,
as if school had let
out: her husband watched
her till loosened away himself
for care: then,

seeming to know but never
quite sure, she was put in
a slightly less hopeful
setting: she watched her
husband tremble in to call

and shoot up high head-bent
eyes: her mind
flashed clear through, she was
sure of it, she had seen
that one before: her husband

longed to say goodbye or else
hello, but the room stiffened
as if two lovers had just caught
on sight, every move rigid
misfire in that perilous fire.

. . . .

Late Look

The last one
died and she
shook with relief,

her house free
from the threat of
sick old people

only to see in
the mirror an
old woman arriving.

I Went Back

I went back
to my old home
and the furrow
of each year
plowed like
surf across
the place had
not washed
memory away.

. . . .

Wiring

Radiance comes from
on high and, staying,
sends down silk
lines to the flopping
marionette, me, but
love comes from
under the ruins and
sends the lumber up
limber into leaf that
touches so high it nearly
puts out the radiance

. . . .

The Role of Society in the Artist

Society sent me this invitation to go to
hell and
delighted not to be overlooked I thought

I could make arrangements to accommodate
it and went off
where, however, I

did the burning by myself, developing
fortunately some fairly thick shields
against blazing and some games

one of which was verse by which I used
illusion to put the flames out,
turning flares into mirrors

of seeming: society
attracted to this bedazzlement wanted me
to acknowledge how it had been

largely responsible and I said oh yes it gave
me the language by which to send me
clear invitations and society

designated me of social value and lifted me
out of hell so I could better share
paradisal paradigms with it

and it said isn't it generous
of society to let you walk here
far from hell—society does this because

it likes your keen sense of acquired sight
& word: how wonderful of you to say so, I said,
and took some of whatever was being

passed around but every night went out
into the forest to spew fire
that blazoned tree trunks and set

stumps afire and society found me out there
& warmed itself and said it liked my unconventional
verses best & I invited society to go to hell

Trigger

I almost step on
a huge spider:
it stalls and
disperses
like oil-beads on water,
baby spiders
shedding radially
till a skinny
mother hardly
shades the
spent center.

. . . .

Dusk Water

Looks like, the rain run off, the brook's
pane-deep again and
over the flat shale-squares
hardly blurs to move:

bushes overhang (small trout floating
leaf-still in hollows) but
I can see when
the catbird lights in, his skinny

feet cracking the mirror,
and then follows so much
shattering and splinter-flicking! which
though when he

stops wet to look around,
melts back, all the rag
beads and quivers and the small mist,
to double-bird fine glass.

Windy Morning with a Little Sleet

The roar of the wind coming
gets here before the wind

doing sixty does and the airy
billows sizzling fry rolling

uphill from the lake till
tugging and tearing they

fall on our flat walls and poor
bushes: I wish we had left

the trees on this continent
up, but then there would have

been too many wolves and timber
rattlers: still, the streams

would have been as constant
and clear as diamonds, and

the wind probably would have
been as soft as *bough* sounds:

poor shrubs & bushes, scant
borders of ice-slick fields,

what a scraggly fringe you make
against this stripped harrowing,

the naked wind, where once in
the cathedral of trees the

turrets would have stirred only
to bedazzle bits of
sunlight on the prayer-still floor.

Singling & Doubling Together

My nature singing in me is your nature singing:
you have means to veer down, filter through,
and, coming in,
harden into vines that break back with leaves,
so that when the wind stirs
I know you are there and I hear you in leafspeech,

though of course back into your heightenings I
can never follow: you are there beyond
tracings flesh can take,
and farther away surrounding and informing the systems,
you are as if nothing, and
where you are least knowable I celebrate you most

or here most when near dusk the pheasant squawks and
lofts at a sharp angle to the roost cedar,
I catch in the angle of that ascent,
in the justness of that event your pheasant nature,
and when dusk settles, the bushes creak and
snap in their natures with your creaking

and snapping nature: I catch the impact and turn
it back: cut the grass and pick up branches
under the elm, rise to the several tendernesses
and griefs, and you will fail me only as from the still
of your great high otherness you fail all things,
somewhere to lift things up, if not those things again:

even you risked all the way into the taking on of shape
and time fail and fail with me, as me,
and going hence with me know the going hence
and in the cries of that pain it is you crying and
you know of it and it is my pain, my tears, my loss—
what but grace

have I to bear in every motion,
embracing or turning away, staggering or standing still,
while your settled kingdom sways in the distillations of light
and plunders down into the darkness with me
and comes nowhere up again but changed into your
singing nature when I need sing my nature nevermore.

. . . .

MAYA ANGELOU

Country Lover

Funky blues
Keen toed shoes
High water pants
Saddy night dance
Red soda water
and anybody's daughter

. . . .

A Good Woman Feeling Bad

The blues may be the life you've led
Or midnight hours in
An empty bed. But persecuting
Blues I've known
Could stalk
Like tigers, break like bone,

Pend like rope in
A gallows tree,
Make me curse
My pedigree,

Bitterness thick on
A rankling tongue,
A psalm to love that's
Left unsung,

Rivers heading north
But ending South,
Funeral music
In a going-home mouth.

All riddles are blues,
And all blues are sad,
And I'm only mentioning
Some blues I've had.

. . . .

Momma Welfare Roll

Her arms semaphore fat triangles,
Pudgy hands bunched on layered hips
Where bones idle under years of fatback
And lima beans.
Her jowls shiver in accusation
Of crimes clichéd by
Repetition. Her children, strangers
To childhood's toys, play
Best the games of darkened doorways,
Rooftop tag, and know the slick feel of
Other people's property.

Too fat to whore,
Too mad to work,
Searches her dreams for the
Lucky sign and walks bare-handed
Into a den of bureaucrats for
Her portion.
"They don't give me welfare.
I take it."

. . . .

Contemporary Announcement

Ring the big bells,
cook the cow,
put on your silver locket.
The landlord is knocking at the door
and I've got the rent in my pocket.

Douse the lights,
hold your breath,
take my heart in your hand.
I lost my job two weeks ago
and rent day's here again.

. . . .

Amoebaean for Daddy

I was a pretty baby.
White folks used to stop
My mother
Just to look at me.
(All black babies
Are Cute). Mother called me
Bootsie and Daddy said . . .
(Nobody listened to him).

On the Union Pacific, a
Dining-car waiter, bowing and scraping,
Momma told him to
Stand up straight, he shamed her
In the big house
(Bought from tips) in front of her
Nice club ladies.

His short legs were always
Half bent. He could have posed as
The Black jockey Mother found
And put on the lawn.
He sat silent when
We ate from the good railroad china
And stolen silver spoons.
Furniture crowded our
Lonely house.

But I was young and played
In the evenings under a blanket of
Licorice sky. When Daddy came home
(I might be forgiven) that last night,
I had been running in the
Big back yard and
Stood sweating above the tired old man,
Panting like a young horse,
Impatient with his lingering. He said
"All I ever asked, all I ever asked, all I ever—"
Daddy, you should have died
Long before I was a
Pretty baby, and white
Folks used to stop
Just to look at me.

. . . .

Preacher, Don't Send Me

Preacher, don't send me
when I die
to some big ghetto
in the sky
where rats eat cats
of the leopard type
and Sunday brunch
is grits and tripe.

I've known those rats
I've seen them kill
and grits I've had
would make a hill,
or maybe a mountain,
so what I need
from you on Sunday
is a different creed.

Preacher, please don't
promise me
streets of gold
and milk for free.
I stopped all milk
at four years old
and once I'm dead
I won't need gold.

I'd call a place
pure paradise
where families are loyal
and strangers are nice,
where the music is jazz
and the season is fall.
Promise me that
or nothing at all.

. . . .

Why Are They Happy People?

Skin back your teeth, damn you,
wiggle your ears,
laugh while the years
race
down your face.

Pull up your cheeks, black boy,
wrinkle your nose,
grin as your toes
spade
up your grave.

Roll those big eyes, black gal,
rubber your knees,
smile when the trees
bend
with your kin.

The Memory

Cotton rows crisscross the world
    And dead-tired nights of yearning
Thunderbolts on leather strops
    And all my body burning

Sugar cane reach up to God
    And every baby crying
Shame the blanket of my night
    And all my days are dying

Les Todd, Duke Photo Department

. . . .

JAMES APPLEWHITE

Some Words for Fall

The tobacco's long put in. Whiffs of it curing
Are a memory that rustles the sweet gums.
Pete and Joe paid out, maybe two weeks ago.
The way their hard hands hook a bottle of Pepsi Cola,
It always makes me lonesome for something more.
The language they speak is things to eat.
Barbeque's smell shines blue in the wind.
Titles of Nehi Grape, Doctor Pepper, are nailed
Onto barns, into wood sides silvered and alive,
Like the color pork turns in heat over ashes.

I wish I could step through the horizon's frame
Into a hand-hewn dirt-floored room.
People down home in Eastern N.C.,
When they have that unlimited longing,
They smell the packhouse leavings.
They look at leaves like red enamel paint
On soft drink signs by the side of the road
That drunks in desperation have shot full of holes.
No words they have are enough.
Sky in rags between riverbank trees
Pieces the torn banner of a heroic name.

. . . .

Tobacco Men

Late fall finishes the season for marketing:
Auctioneers babble to growers and buyers.
Pickups convoy on half-flat tires, tobacco
Piled in burlap sheets, like heaped-up bedding
When sharecropper families move on in November.

No one remembers the casualties
Of July's fighting against time in the sun.
Boys bent double for sand lugs, bowed
Like worshippers before the fertilized stalks.
The rubber-plant leaves glared savagely as idols.

It is I, who fled such fields, who must
Reckon up losses: Walter fallen out from heat,
Bud Powell nimble along rows as a scatback
But too light by September, L. G. who hoisted up a tractor
To prove he was better, while mud hid his feet—
I've lost them in a shimmer that makes the rows move crooked.

Wainwright welded the wagons, weighed three
Hundred pounds, and is dead. Rabbit was mechanic
When not drunk, and Arthur best ever at curing.
Good old boys together—maybe all three still there,
Drinking in a barn, their moonshine clearer than air
Under fall sky impenetrable as a stone named for azure.

I search for your faces in relation
To a tobacco stalk I can see,
One fountain of up-rounding leaf.
It looms, expanding, like an oak.
Your faces form fruit where branches are forking.
Like the slow-motion explosion of a thunderhead,
It is sucking the horizon to a bruise.

A cloud's high forehead wears ice.

· · · · · · ·

A Vigil

I
Thanksgiving sacrament, piety of crystal and silver.
Platters and dishes passed on from hand to hand.
Words so well-worn they drone with the summertime fan.
My grandfather blessing, his countenance fields in the sunlight.

I waited beside him for words, for what he'd gathered
From hawks wheeling sun, oak leaves' tension under glare.
He rocked in the parlor with a bible, his face grown taciturn,
The hooked nose indian, hair as if filamented down.
His parchment skin was the season's hieroglyphic.
Going for water, I passed through the company parlor:
Mantle with mirror and clock, stiff plush and varnish.

II

One window overlooked the trees of the creek, where silt
From high water on leaves seemed dust from the passing days.

I poured from a pitcher. Tracing a beaded trickle,
Sweat down a frosted tumbler. Sensation of October
In August. I thirsted to bring into potable solution
These motes of dust that swam the green shade's sunbeam.
I sat on the porch beside him, spell-bound by columns.
Horizon woven to softening by orbits of swallows.

"It's been eighty-six years and it seems like a day."

. . . .

Barbecue Service

I have sought the elusive aroma
Around outlying cornfields, turned corners
Near the site of a Civil War surrender.
The transformation may take place
At a pit no wider than a grave,
Behind a single family's barn.
These weathered ministers
Preside with the simplest of elements:
Vinegar and pepper, split pig and fire.
Underneath a glistening mountain in air,
Something is converted to a savor: the pig
Flesh purified by far atmosphere.
Like the slick-sided sensation from last summer,

A fish pulled quick from a creek
By a boy. Like breasts in a motel
With whiskey and twilight
Now a blue smoke in memory.
This smolder draws the soul of our longing.

I want to see all the old home folks,
Ones who may not last another year.
We will rock on porches like chapels
And not say anything, their faces
Impenetrable as different barks of trees.
After the brother who drank has been buried,
The graveplot stunned by sun
In the woods,
We men still living pass the bottle.
We barbecue pigs.
The tin-roofed sheds with embers
Are smoking their blue sacrifice
Across Carolina.

. . . .

Collards

Green hens perching the pole
    Of a row, concentric wings
Fly you down into soil.

You catch the rain like rings
    Where a pine stump tunnels
Time backward down roots' seasonings.

If roots rot to dark channels
    Mining the forest, your fiber
Threads grease in the entrails

Of families, whose bodies harbor
Scars like rain on a hillslope,
Whose skin takes sheen like lumber

Left out in the weather. Old folk
Seem sewed together by pulp
Of your green rope and smoke

From the cook fires boys gulp
For dinner along roads in winter.
Collards and ham grease they drop

In the pot come back as we enter
The house whose porch shows a pumpkin.
This steam holds all we remember.

Sweet potatoes clot in a bin,
Common flesh beneath this skin
Like collards. Grainy-sweet, kin.

.   .   .   .

Greene County Pastoral

I hope that Mary Alice Philips who lived
by the river will pick new
jonquils for the casket.

Maybe L. G. Newcomb whose four-room house
stood in a bend of the creek road
will come with a fist of forsythia.

I wish the girls and boys I knew, from creekside and
mule lot, from rosy broom sedge knolls,
could start past edges of pine woods.

I think their singing and sighing might rustle
      with the needles and hush like the dove
          wings alighting on light wires

On hills far away in the country. Their preachers
      might come looking pale and fresh-shaven
          from the white inside the wooden churches.

May their sermons on sin and punishment subside,
      let them calm those waters. Let Jesus walk
          out of their words and pass among

L. G.'s crowd where they're turning the reel in the Contentnea.
      Let his face be from faces in the boats on
          the Neuse, the Pamlico, the Cape Fear.

Those who drowned, let them arise.
      The white face of one from underwater
          will still these troubles. While they

Scoop up nets full of shad and cats and their
      campfire flickers more orange as the sun
          goes down, may the mules

In the fenced lots hang their heads sorrowfully
      and turn their hindquarters to the wind,
          one hoof scraping a corn cob.

May wind through dog fennel of the deserted
      pasture sway the soft weeds just at the tips
          so they touch the fence's wire.

May the sky and the land be one in evening,
      the pale light a lake for the straw
          and the twigs and the weeds

And fish in the reel and the horses and mules
   and Mary Alice Philips and L. G.,
      and Christ like a drowned man arisen.

Let the deserted house with scrolled cornices
   in the grove of broken oaks with a few
      jonquils spotting that shadow

Be circled like an elegy by swallows.
   Let them know that she always loved them.
      Let this light and these fields

Hold her spirit as naturally as a straw
   basket carries the loose flowers.
      Let the light in that cloud fade to stone.

May she lie at peace with the forsythia, spirea, willow
   brought her by bare-footed farm girls
      in my frail thoughts' pastoral.

. . . .

A Leaf of Tobacco

Is veined with mulatto hands. The ridges extending
Along crests of the topographical map from the stem
Marking a mountainous ridge encounter wrinkles
Where streams lead down toward coastal pocosins.
This time-yellowed scrap of a partial history
Features humans driven on like mules with no reprisal.
The grit your fingers feel exploring this pungent terrain
Is fragments of a Staffordshire tea service
Buried from Sherman in fields near Bentonville.
The snuff-colored resin on the ball of your finger
Crystallized in the corners of seventy-five-year-old lips,
On the porch of a shotgun shack, as she watched her grandsons
Crop lugs on their knees in the sun. This leaf has collected,
Like a river system draining a whole basin,

The white organdy lead bullet coon dog Baptist
Preacher iron plough freed slave raped and
Bleeding dead from the lynch mob cotton
Mouth South. Scented and sweetened with rum and molasses,
Rolled into cigarettes or squared in a thick plug,
Then inhaled or chewed, this history is like syrupy
Moonshine distilled through a car radiator so the salts
Strike you blind. Saliva starts in the body. We die for this leaf.

. . . .

Earth Lust

Sirened by a wind, we who belong
Here go out picking or digging, drawn
By berries past purple: the blisters' strong
Skins along the stems of thorn.
We who rupture these sweets with the tongue
Have suffered the ticks', the chiggers' penalties,
Can see beneath the three-leaved spray
To a poison inside our own bodies.
It boils up, answering the ivy's oil.

I am called again to a homestead's soil
Deep in woods, where periwinkle spread
In a green counterpane over the dead
Is irresistible. I have to go dig
Where vines and spiderwebs bind my head
Till I am dizzy in the heat, lose control,
Grab up all I can carry in a roll:
Like a live blanket to make my own bed.
Ivy-coil fangs my arms and legs.

We southerners must survive an embrace
Of briars, a thirst for a touch of earth
Too rough for love. For us born here, a poisonous
Juice scalds both sides of the fence of skin.
The soil is extended family, larger twin,

Relative forgotten in trees as the split rails
Rot down, till only periwinkle calls
Some son back to the hug that stings—
Past snake's skin, the blackberry strings.

. . . .

Southern Voices

If you understand my accent,
You will know it is not out of ignorance.
Broom sedge in wind has curved this bent
Into speech. This clay of vowels, this diffidence

Of consonantal endings, murmurs *defeat*:
Caught like a chorus from family and servants.
This is the hum of blessings over the meat
Your cavalry spared us, echoed from an aunt's

Bleak pantry. This colorless tone, like flour
Patted onto the cheeks, is poor-white powder
To disguise the minstrel syllables lower
In our register, from a brownface river.

If it sounds as if minds were starved,
Maybe fatback and beans, yams and collards
Weighed down vitamins of wit, lard
Mired speed, left wetlip dullards

In cabins by cotton. But if bereft
Of the dollars and numbers, our land's whole
Breath stirs with Indian rivers. Our cleft
Palate waters for a smoke of the soul,

A pungence of pig the slaves learned
To burn in pits by the levee. This melon
Round of field and farmer, servant turned
Tenant, longs for a clear pronunciation,

But stutters the names of governors, Klan
And cross-burnings, mad dogs and lynchings.
So ours is the effacing slur of men
Ashamed to speak. We suffer dumb drenchings

Of honeysuckle odor, love for a brother
Race which below the skin is us, lust
Projected past ego onto this shadow-other.
So we are tongue-tied, divided, the first

To admit face to face our negligence
And ignorance of self: our musical tone
Of soul-syllable, penchant for the past tense,
Harelip contractions unable to be one.

. . . .

Summer Revival

The revival preacher journeyed us night and day,
Behind the pillar of fire and cloud. Outside, where
The churchyard oak held up its limbs to a streetlight's
Judgment, moths seemed the fantasies it brooded.
But these wings were nothing beside his Angel of Death.
We each felt ourselves firstborn, wished
To splatter any lintel (was it doorway or post?)
With our blood. Kneeling before Abraham's knife,
We looked about for the ram with the tangled horns.
But the bush that was burning was the unconsumed
Wicker of our veins. Not even the plagued, Passover night
Could quench it. We sucked in the iron commandments.
The apple still dripping was snatched from our lips,
Was replaced by a Word inscribed as on a stone
From Sinai. We traveled a wilderness bound
For no temporal conclusion. Jerusalem was henceforth
Abstracted in air, built by an alabaster rhetoric,
Of substances we knew only as sounds: sword names,
Edged with prohibition. The solace for judgment

Would be a final judgment, when a hand
Would shear us, bleating elegiacs, from the other,
Pan-footed flock. We shuffled the rain-blackened
Sidewalk, our leather heels hard as hooves.

. . . .

White Lake

Rimmed in by cypresses, tin water flashed
Like the top of a can, in fields still buzzing
With cicadas: electrical August short-circuiting.
The surface slicked over us like oil, shone
Silver with clouds. We walked, holding hands,
Toward the rides: Roller Coaster. Dive Bomber.
We sat in the Ferris Wheel, throbbing
With its engine, as it hurried us backward,
To show a black polish, the lake like marble
Under stars, bulbs on its opposite shore
Rolling across reflection in miniature pearls.

With a wince of thrill in the quick of our spines,
We offered up ourselves to a turning as enormous
As the seasons or desire, whirled down to search
Shadows, where water lapped subtly at roots,
For a place we could lie down together, wandered
Through glare from the lighted piers,
Till we took our chances below a capsized boat.
In the rides park afterward, there were dolls
To be won by rings or thrown balls.
Pandas, like drunken guests at a wedding,
Formal in their black and white, faced
A tree-tall whirling as if spun by a giant.

The Descent

You must drive to these little towns
(Appie, or Seven Springs)
Expecting nothing.
You must find in the general store
More than you came for
These olives in glass, deviled ham in tins
These letters of labels
As from the box of eight crayons—
Colors of the new alphabet
That once outlined first figure
On canvas empty as a mirror.
Then, you couldn't imagine yet
How light would be bent, and wet.
How birdsong would be muted
And your innocence learn the sordid
Involvement with its new vesture:
Each fold and slit of the creature.
So this was the descent of the soul
You say, buying a ginger ale.
This is as it was when you were young.
This was the shelved house
Holding all experience for the mouth.
The Japanese paper umbrellas were next door.
White lattice upon the second floor
Made your prison bars, a porch
Like a first grade stool
Where your bird soul could perch
And practice its song of flutter
And fall, thrusting its tongue
Into darknesses like molasses.
Oh these towns, these elementary classes.
You pause on the sheltered walk,
For a moment in the pane
Of that earlier world, when all
Was excruciating, pristine.

The car you drive is a kind of burial.
You promise yourself to come again.

. . . .

News of Pearl Harbor

From the arched Philco with its speaker like a Gothic window
    came news from the sky. Later, newsreels showed the *Arizona*
hulled over, burning. The P-40's and slender-tailed B-17's in
    their peacetime markings lay crumpled in piles. The sky
became accelerator of change—no longer the river with
    its slow hieroglyphic, its evolution from sailing craft
and log raft to steam-huffed packet. Not the railroad
    with its comprehensible, coal-fired engine in its black
piston-shape, not even the new year's models of Chryslers
    and Buicks, but an airborne sound from the distance: Pearl
Harbor, jewel-lustrous, catastrophic syllables. Volunteers
    watched from Forest Service tower and rooftop, with manuals
to aid them, though the middle-aged eyes behind glasses confused one
    aircraft with another. But the boy on the roof of his father's
station recognized each type as by instinct—in the one-room
    house all windows, as he waited for apocalyptic sightings.
He imagined a desperate combat the whole country entered in,
    his somnolent South now wired by the phone line that
began at his own left hand to the military fathers, whose
    planes changed as quickly as the broadcasts: P-38's and
B-17's, the milk-jug P-47's, moving through the new marks,
    with armor and self-sealing tanks, machine guns and
cannon, stabilizer-fins extended. Young men training
    at Seymour Johnson nearby strained to learn control
of a fighter like a winged locomotive. One of these P-47's
    crashed in the edge of his county. He went with his father.
The boulderlike motor had broken from its mounts, an engine
    of two thousand horsepower rolling like the Juggernaut of
wartime, bowling down pine trees, letting in sunlight
    through the central, violated grove, toward the hollow,
frangible body. This Thunderbolt of a technical rhetoric

in a pastoral accumulated too vividly for scrutiny
illuminated a fuselage broken at the cockpit: a pilot's
	seat stark as an electric chair, where the throne
of this new succession stood jellied with blood.

.　.　.　.　.　.　.　.

My Cousin Sue's Broad View

Rolling her neck upon the ladder back
	of chair she curved her eyes toward air
that freshened west beyond the porch, a torch
	upon her skin where sun fell plumb from
shingles hung like bangs. I couldn't gauge
	her years from eyes or from her widely open
arc of mouth, that lipped horizoned earth from west
	to east, from pine grove nested sharp and dense
to furrows and sparrows along a barbed-wire fence.
	She lolled her tongue and gasped as if her mirth
could swallow all sweet and sour of birth like biscuits
	with buttermilk. Her sister's gaze lay on us both,
lines of mouth like wire toward me but soft as her dog's
	fur for Sue, who sweltered like bread under cloth
and cursed with cleft lip in a voice that missed
	no note the choir might touch, whose body's slouch
was matched to porch and air and the sun's pouring
	and my pleasure beyond reason that July morning.
I'd come to my cousin's, his sister surprised at ease
	with the farm in her arms, that she spread
to an unembarrassed sky, plumply at home
	though her brain was said by some to be strange.
Yet for me she was large and wise as she smiled
	upon the privilege of being, that had no edge
they could push you over while you lived, no void
	to be harried into, nothing to snatch at thatches
of your hair if straw like hers, or if mine,
	like fallen needles of pine. They couldn't stop
her laugh or say she didn't belong: strong in

her innocence, like the blank air from whence swallows
twittered later, wiggling wings, making jokes of grace.

. . . .

The Cemetery next to Contentnea

Births and deaths were at home. Farm wives bore
    children in double beds, whose mattresses remembered
their conceptions—birth stains and death stains never
    entirely washed from pads and quilts. And though farm-
hardy, one or more of the ten or twelve would not survive—
    what with flu, scarlet fever, whooping cough, mumps,
infections when all the doctor would do was puncture
    the eardrum. With his black snap bag in his buggy,
the doctor was little more help than the preacher. Midwives
    delivered babies, neighbor women who knew how to tie
off the cord and cut it, who had talked the mother through
    the worst pain, and now handed her the red little
face just squeezed out like a pea between fingers.
    People lived and died as their destiny let them;
home remedies placated rashes with boiled peach
    leaves or a dusting of cornmeal, and fat meat
with a drop of turpentine would draw out the splinter.
    The close-fitting belly band held in the infant's navel,
and purgations with castor oil seemed a punishment
    and forgiveness of the body. Life was statistical,
for those left after the night-agony, when a wind seemed
    rushing through the house, the oil lamps flickering
at the end. All linens would be boiled and the room
    opened up to the air, the floor and the walls scrubbed.
The raw earth in a graveplot on a rise across the road
    showed a mound that would settle over years. Gradually
medicine grew helpful, with ether for setting broken bones,
    vaccinations for smallpox, diphtheria, typhoid fever.
Survivable operations began to be performed in hospitals
    in small cities: Wilson, Goldsboro, New Bern, places
of last resort, where the grief-stricken couple might take

their screaming child in their new automobile late
at night: museumlike corridors smelling of disinfectant.
    People who had faced birth and death straight on took
parents and children to these houses of collective mourning,
    and let the white screens, the gauzes, bandage away sight
of the vagina that gaped after birth, blood trickling out of it;
    of the convulsive throes and gasps of final breaths.
But farm folk continued to surround the dying, like
    the birth giving, with a family presence, waiting in
couples and cross-generational groupings in the public lobbies,
    standing in the corridor outside the door at the end,
coming in for a last hoarse word, a hand-squeeze, a kiss
    with dry lips. And the funerals in white wooden churches
with graveside services kept on, even if the buried
    were no longer in plots in the fields, stones squared away
from the corn by fences—wrought iron softened by rust,
    no longer as hard as the blackberry bramble around it.

. . . .

GERALD BARRAX

Something I Know about Her

She touches when she talks—
must touch to smooth out syntax with her fingertips,
must lay on her hand to hear her echo,
to feel the words you don't speak
below the ones you do.

What she means by it is warm;
if she touches you, listen:
to surprise her at it
   would be like waking a sleepwalker
   between two dreams—
would trap her in this tedious
world of mere jive words.

. . . .

Body Food

Oh my Brothers
you who need it
it is your right
to turn to what
you believe is the true
God or any other
but what do you think
kept your great & grand
papas & mamas alive long
& strong enough to give you
the strength to make the choice?:
to take a faith with roots
which their spirits yearned back for
while their blood hallowed
the cradles out of which your flesh
came into this wilderness?
   You their children
know better than the masters

who were ignorant of the strength it took
to begin with to survive;
what little they had was given grudgingly
without the suspicion of what
those strong men & strong
women could make of leavings.

   If then it is in the blood of some of us
to lust after the ears the tails the snouts
the feet the maws & even the
chitlins of the filthy beast
forgive us: with these
& the greens cornbread & molasses
that transubstantiated into the bones
brain & flesh of the black household gods
who brought us through the evil
rooted in this land,
   we honor them
in the heritage of their strength.

. . . .

Another Fellow

The almost whole skin
Lay right outside the window of my basement
Where I'd been entombed for more than a year.
Whenever it happened, if I had raised myself
And looked out of the groundlevel window
I'd have seen it crawling out of its year-old skin;
It would've seen a face marveling and envious
Up from a book behind the screen,
But it would've been too busy
Doing what it was supposed to do
To stop for me;
My ancestors, considering its immortality,
Would've welcomed it with food and drink
When it came as spirit of the living-dead from the forest
To visit their huts;

And I would've sacrificed a book to its wisdom
In return for a poem.
 Dear Emily,
That was in September, months ago.
The grass after days of rain was high, wet, still growing
And had to be cut once more for the year. I cut it
In anticipation, wondering if I would drive it
Into the square of the yard, or out,
Half dreading both but needing
One or the other. This year I will be 43.
I found neither the spotted shaft in the high grass
Nor in my room your worm transformed
And ringed with power. I found an empty skin
That I threw over the fence.

. . . .

Who Needs No Introduction

Sometimes in the cool of the garden
he walks through the setting that was
his early and, some say, only
success; the birds, flowers, animals
and all the rest whose names he can't
always remember still there,
properties for another try. He picks,
examines a strawberry in amazement, watches
the way the sun comes and goes,
the seasons of the moon. He thinks they
serve him better than the myriad little
theaters that sprang up like weeds
in old gardens and put on
those amateurish spectacles in his name.
The rivalry between them was killing—each
company with its prescribed repertory of roles,
masks, rituals—none of it adding
to his stature. It was all so wearying.

Bursting out of the dew
he loafs with snails under the leaves,
admiring the warm sound their moist
muscles make as they go; or listens
in disbelief to a mad mockingbird,
unable to recall the sanity or the whim
in which he had done that. He imagines
that he had stopped there the first
time, and leans against the grass
in the spotlight of his last star.

· · · · · · · ·

Spirituals, Gospels

Nothing on earth can make me believe them.
I cringe before the weary forgiving
of that lord whose blood whose blood drowned our gods,
who survived the slave pens
where, thrown in by the masters
as bait to control the chattel,
they nevertheless took him, made him blacker
almost than the masters could endure.
Yet still today, still they sing
to be washed white in his glory, sing
of a bitter earth where my confusions deceive me
   with sweet seasons at my door,
    with dream or memory of savanna and plain
     where the lord is elephant and lion;
      jungle where the deaths of lesser gods
        feed back into its own resurrection;
      canopied rainforest, all that life in the trees
as this earth's heaven.
And whales sing in our oceans.

Yet my own blood weakens, freezes
at their sound, the "unearthly harmonies"
alone probing the faith in my doubt,

making me fear the joy that for the duration of the music
crushes resistance utterly, utterly.
And I know that's who I am, what I am
when the souls of Black folk sing.
While the Soul of Black folk sings.

. . . .

One More Word

The universe already thrashes
in a big fishnet of words
because everybody thinks nothing is
and nothing had without a name

so I named her a word
that hummed in the wetness of a bad night
because she was escapable
and undiscoverable

as the universe in a fishnet
and my hands were wet for her
but the naming was as good
as when God said

"Give them names Adam"
and Adam named
better than anyone ever
until I named her Lover

in a bad night blowing wetness
and the universe kicked at the net
in a storm
and the thunder said Never.

Two Figures on Canvas

Here in this foreground of sunny Italian fields
She accepts exile as obligation to art.
This one, as all the others,
Has brought her here for his own need
From her harsher land beyond those background towers
Where even a stable and clean straw served
The kind of need they all understand.
He smiles in appreciation at his image of her.
And she, in spirit, must smile because she is aware
Of her renascence among women,
And is woman enough to smile.

She takes and comforts the child.
She assumes her pose from habit, endurance.
She accepts the gambit of heavy satin gown
In fashion with a wistful fancy
For the extravagant cascade of solemn Latin and feudal music:
But she laughs at his need for those moons,
For those pancake haloes.

. . . .

Portraits

On the four-to-twelve shift
on the open door of a locker
a pinktipped kneeling nude
cups, lifts, and squeezes her
self in hands too small
for her own abundance of glossy goodness.
Her smile is warm, sincere.
She is perfectly innocent.
Scotchtaped below her
is a longhaired man with the saddest
blue eyes, too much a gentleman to look up,
but innocently ahead, his hands

pointing the eye to the exposed
incredibly red dripping heart.
He is perfectly serious.
Who wouldn't be proud of a daughter like that?
What a blessing to have such a son.

. . . .

Liberation

It's one of those little mean
Coincidences our world turns on.
Only last night I read Sexton's
Celebration of her uterus,
And here I am this
Morning, sitting by
Without use in my wife's room
While the surgeons' hands work busily
Removing hers. And I celebrate
That sacred part of her
That has withstood, for mere human love,
The trials and crucifixions of her body.
Miscarriage and birth and
Miscarriage and birth and
Pain, and pain. I always said
"We" lost the baby, just as I said "We"
Have a daughter, but I could say nothing
About that pain. She lay there
In the middle of it, while I
Could only stumble
Around its
Edges,
Terrified of its
Vaguest touch. At the ends of our dark nights
Together, after her pain had shriveled
My little mortal soul to dust,
I could never decide which made the crueler joke:
God as male bungler

Or God as female masochist.
But the survivors were women,
She and the two Lovelies
Who clung to that sacred part
For mere human love, and were delivered.

And I celebrate that woman
Who stood bleeding two years
On her magnificent pillars
Like another wonder,
Bleeding her human blood,
Baptizing me as I crawled under her,
My belly lower than the ground.

And God, dam the blood of the lamb.
I celebrate the merely human bleeding womb
That brought salvation to us all.

. . . .

Domestic Tranquility

I need a ritual to perform,
clean and sane, for this perfect washday,
the sun burning the top of my head
and forearms raised to the line,
the surrogate wind breathing
my wife's blouses, my daughters' dresses and jeans.
I need a formula to recite
free of mumbo jumbo and cant,
as fit for me and this day, and I say
to hell with Kenmore, Whirlpool, Maytag,
who needs Norge, Wards, Westinghouse, GE?

When I strung my clothesline from the post
where the rosebush fans over the redwood fence,
I was careful not to scare the rabbit away,
come to the yard for clover,

crouching on the cool ground along the fence
among the mint that's grown high as my knee;
it sits in there still and breathless with revelation,
the laundry like sweet apparitions flapping overhead,
my presence humming through the intoxicating leaves.
I wish that kind of myth to give my daughters,
as free of cruelty and lies
as the vision of this small waiting animal.
Today I have only this day so perfect for the wash
drying by sun and wind, and a miracle for the rabbit
at peace under the rose bush.

. . . .

Theology

Driving five-year-old Dara to school December 15,
she tells me that God was visible
when he created the world,
but that made him tired,
so he died,
and went to heaven,
then he became invisible.

Suddenly *I* understand Lao-Tzu, Plato,
Augustine and Aquinas,
Barth, Tillich,
all those guys—

the whole thing.

. . . .

Strangers Like Us: Pittsburgh, Raleigh, 1945–1985

The sounds our parents heard echoing over
housetops while listening to evening radios
were the uninterrupted cries running and cycling

we sent through the streets and yards, where spring summer
fall we were entrusted to the night, boys
and girls together, to send us home for bath
and bed after the dark had drifted down and eased
contests between pitcher and batter, hider and seeker.

Our own children live imprisoned in light.
They are cycloned into our yards and hearts,
whose gates flutter shut on unfamiliar smiles.
At the rumor of a moon, we call them in
before the monsters who hunt, who hurt, who haunt
us, rise up from our own dim streets.

. . . .

What More?

My lawnmower has awakened the resident god of my yard
who rubs its leafy hand in anticipation
of troubling me again with one of its cruel koans,

this one a small bird dropped
from the sky, or thrown out,
out of the sweetgum tree

where I was cutting
that long triangle of grass outside
the back fence: put there

when I wasn't looking, it lies
on its back twitching half in and out of the swath
I cut a minute before.

I'm being tampered with again,
like an electron whose orbit and momentum
are displaced by the scientist's measurement

and observation. If I'd found something already stiff
and cold on the ground
I'd have kicked or nudged it out of my path:

but the just-dead, the thing still warm,
just taken its last breath, made its last
movement, has its own kind of horror.

I leave the small patch of uncut grass around it.
Back inside my enclosed yard
I see a brown thrasher come and stand over the body,

with some kind of food in its bill.
(I was careful to say "bill" and not "mouth.")
By the next time I cut myself around the yard,

I see the thrasher sitting on the fence above the still dead,
still holding whatever it has in its bill. I've described
it all accurately. What more could anyone expect of me?

. . . .

Haunted House

1.
The smallest bones in Helen's body
Don't dampen amplitudes as they should,
And, deep inside, her ears hurt. Her drums
Are set at such exquisite tension against my music
That a few measures from a sonata
Or a lyric I thought I'd forgot
Invites someone I loved or wanted
Forty years ago to take me back, away,
While she is distracted by threshold pain,
And makes the house tremble with her complaint
Against the noise,
However quietly my deference plays for her.

2.

I've memorized dozens of songs, old
Now, and must be the last man alive
Who remembers the Four Tunes
And Savannah Churchill, and knows the words
To "Is It Too Late?" and "I Understand,"
At thirteen the first record I bought.
I thought my voice was good enough,
But girls wondered, "Who is this strange
Boy singing to me?" They were charmed
But found it uncomfortable
And too odd to risk.
I married the first woman who didn't think so,
Who steered me arm in arm
Singing down dark streets
"The Nearness of You," who tried with me
My weird pastime of reading through
Ellington and Verdi scores.
But divorced and died away from that music,
I brought my life away on reels of taped 78s.

3.

I sing to no one in this house,
Except alone, except to ghosts.
At the piano or stereo I cram
Eighth notes into my mouth with both
Hands, delight in the bite of their comet
Tails; sprinkle black pepper Thirty-
Seconds on my grits, crunchy crouton
Sixteenths on salads, make perfect Martinis
With black olive Quarter notes;
The powerful head-clearing Half note mints
Like the days of creation, prepare me
For the Whole, the cosmic egg,
The singular state of Nommo,
And I don't know that I'm not seeing
Blue Whales swim among the Pleiades when Rachmaninoff
And Ray Charles are transformed to pressure waves

In the liquid Tympani of my inner ear;
When Callas sings, Segovia plays, or Divine Sarah
Divines, I can't swear that I don't hear
The fifty thousand hair cells
Rippling in my organs of Corti as I follow
The electric impulses
Along the thirty thousand fibers of my auditory nerve,
And the brain quadrupling that in numbers of stars
That light folk to goon on galactic pilgrimages
To empty tombs, stones newly rolled away.
And everywhere throughout Andromeda
Young men in castle windows weep
For our loss, for Helen's noise, for Helen's pain.

. . . .

Adagio

That morning you found your lights on,
battery dead, came back to the apartment,
walked in wet and blinking rain at me,
and we went back to the narrow bed

where always I hear the short *Ah!*
when I enter you.
Twenty years, I'll never see you again.
Barber's *Adagio* came six years later.

It's what we wanted for those three months,
for the days I'm going to live with,
like the strings sinking, and sinking:

each time you come back I think
it will be the last time
and I won't know it,
like the last breath I don't remember taking.

· · · · · · · ·

KATHRYN STRIPLING BYER

Wide Open, These Gates

Going down the road feeling good, I snap
my fingers. Hear, hear! At an auction my father
bid sixty-five dollars for a fat Hampshire pig
just by rubbing his nose. When my grandfather
scattered his seed to the four corners, corn stood up
tall as his hat brim. My grandmother's sheets
flapped like bells on the line. Crabbed youth,
crab apple, crepe myrtle, I mumble

as I shuffle downhill, my crabbed youth
behind me like gnats singing. I've come a long way
from what's been described as a mean and starved
corner of backwoods America. That has a ring
to it. Rhythm, like my grandmother's hands
in the bread dough. Her food made the boards creak,
my grandfather mellow. He had a wild temper
when he was a young man. Most folks talk too much,
he'd say, aiming slow spit at a dung beetle.
He never mumbled. Sometimes he talked nonsense

to roosters and fierce setting hens. My nonsense coos
like a dove. Goodbye swallowtails cruising
the pigpen. Goodbye apple dumplings. Goodbye
little turkeys my grandmother fed with her fingers.
Big Belle was a nanny goat. Holler "Halloo"
after sundown and all the cows come home. Some words
are gates swinging wide open, and I walk on through
one more summer that like this road's going
down easy. The gnats sing, and I'm going
to sing. One of these days I'll be gone.

Drought

Dirt, always
the smell of dry dirt
while I sweated through summer,
my father complaining about blue sky
stretching all the way west into Arkansas.
Dry ice they tumbled
from planes sometimes. Thunder
and strong wind might come

but no rain. Pigs grumbled
from sun-up to sundown. The cows stood
immobilized under the oak trees,
their turds turning black as the biscuits I burned
while I daydreamed. Wherever I played I saw corn dying
year after year, teased by dust devils
leaving their tidings between my toes
and in ring after ring round my neck. I scrubbed
ring after ring of black dirt from the bathtub
at night. I got used to my own sweat

and so much hot weather
the fragile petunias collapsed
by mid-afternoon. Hold up
your shoulders straight, I heard a thousand times.
Books on my head, I'd be sent out
to water the flowers as if that would help salvage
anything but my good humor, the smell of wet dirt

my reward, for which I knew I ought
to be grateful, as now nearly twenty years later I am
grateful, thirsty as dry land
I stand upon, stoop-shouldered,
wanting a flash flood to wash away Georgia
while I aim the water hose into a sad patch of pansies.
Nothing has changed. I can still hear my father complain

while my mother cooks supper and I swear to leave
home tomorrow. In some places dams burst
but I don't believe it. Here water is
only illusion, an old trick
light plays on the highway that runs north
through field after field after field.

.   .   .   .

My Beautiful Grandmother

died ugly,
wasted with hunger,
her arms black and blue from the needles,
the last ones she took up
when she stopped embroidering pink cornucopias
on square after square of white cotton.
Nobody could coax her to eat after six years
of morphine. Not even my father.

She'd wanted to leave
for a long time, she wanted
the mountains, the cool
air, the sky coming down
like a good sleep, she wanted

to go back to where she had been
when she wore the red plume in her hat
and sat pointing the toe of her shoe
at the camera. Oh

she was a dashing one
all the men said and say
still if you ask them. Her mind was as quick
as the stitch of a sparrow's wing.
Coming and going,
she made sure her petticoats rustled.
A flirt and a good one she was

and so square-jawed and German she looked
like the belle of some old-country tavern.
Her laugh was a yodel.

She wasn't the belle of that small town
in Georgia. But, stubborn,
she tried what she knew worked
a little while. She fell in love
with a young man whose letters she saved
in a hatbox. I opened one
once. It read: "Darling,
my heart counts the moments
until we are wed!" Then
it crumbled like stale bread.
The rats had gnawed whole words away.
Such a bride,
such a bride, all the townspeople said
and forgot her. I grew up remembering

I was her granddaughter. And it's been years
I've spent leaving that small town in Georgia
where my beautiful grandmother stayed.

. . . .

Angels

We sang Adeste Fideles while
clouds darkened over my grandfather's
farmhouse. What angels
we were, my three cousins caressing
their bride dolls, and I, the soprano
in front keeping time because
I sang the loudest. The nerve
of somebody (my deaf aunt?)
to whisper, "Tornado"! We wouldn't stop
singing till hailstones came
clattering down on the tin roof the way

in the movies Comanches charge out of a hill
like an avalanche. "Open a window,"
my grandfather yelled while we ran
for the root cellar, clutching our candles
like converts. The house howled
with wind as the Angel of Death thundered
on to the next town where (so
it's been told every year since that
Christmas night) two men were raised
by the whirlwind and set down
a mile away, babbling of light
at the end of a tunnel,
the buzzing of ten thousand angels.

. . . .

Kitchen Sink

Today she would change nothing,
not even the wallpaper peeling
like dead bark. Nor, outside, the shadows
approaching the yard where ants
toil like women in their houses of sand.
Never mind that the sun will be setting.

When she was young she felt afraid
of hard wind and the rain that unsettled the creek.
But the earth never left her,
not once did the floods reach her feet.
The reward of a long life is faith

in what's left. Dishes stacked on a strong table.
Jars of dried beans. Scraps of cloth.
And the ten thousand things of her own thoughts,
incessant as creek water. She has been able

to lay up her treasures on earth,
as if heaven were here, worth believing.
In the water her hands reach
like roots grown accustomed to living,

the roots of the cat-briar that hold to the hillside
and can never be torn free of this earth completely.

. . . .

Wildwood Flower

I hoe thawed ground
with a vengeance. Winter has left
my house empty of dried beans
and meat. I am hungry

and now that a few buds appear
on the sycamore, I watch the road
winding down this dark mountain
not even the mule can climb
without a struggle. Long daylight

and nobody comes while my husband
traps rabbits, chops firewood, or
walks away into the thicket. Abandoned
to hoot owls and copperheads,

I begin to fear sickness. I wait
for pneumonia and lockjaw. Each month
I brew squaw tea for pain.
In the stream where I scrub my own blood
from rags, I see all things flow
down from me into the valley.

Once I climbed the ridge
to the place where the sky
comes. Beyond me the mountains continued
like God. Is there no place to hide
from His silence? A woman must work

else she thinks too much. I hoe
this earth until I think of nothing
but the beans I will string,
the sweet corn I will grind into meal.

We must eat. I will learn
to be grateful for whatever comes to me.

. . . .

All Hallows Eve

I go by taper of cornstalk,
the last light of fields wreathed in woodsmoke,
to count the hens left in the chickenhouse
raided by wild dogs and foxes.
Our rooster crows far up the hillside
where three piles of rocks mark the graves
of nobody I ever knew.
Let their ghosts eat him!
Each year they grow hungrier,
wanting the squash run to seed in our garden,
the tough spikes of okra. Tonight while the moon
lays her face on the river and begs
for a love song, they'll come down the mountain
to steal the last apples I've gathered.

They'll stand at the window and ask us
for whom is that buttermilk set on the table?
That platter of cold beans?
They know we will pay them no heed.
It's the wind, we will say,

watching smoke sidle out of the fireplace,
or hearing the cellar door rattle.

No wonder they go away
always complaining how little the living
have learned, on our knees
every night asking God for a clean heart,
a pure spirit. Spirit? They kick
up the leaves round the silent house.
What good is spirit without hands for walnut
to stain, without ears for the river
to fill up with promises? What good,
they whisper, returning to nothing, what good
without tongue to cry out to the moon,
"Thou hast ravished my heart, O my sister!"

. . . .

Lost Soul

Wind shakes the latch on my door
as if someone is knocking.
I stand at the sink, my hands cold

from the clothes I have washed.
On the line they are tossed like lost souls,
and when wind shakes the latch on my door

like a summons, I shut my eyes.
Nightgowns float over the toolshed.
I stand at the sink, my hands cold

and do not fetch them home.
I know better than walk down this mountain
when wind shakes the latch on my door

as if someone is knocking indeed.
Against solitude I have no aid.
Must I stand at the sink, my hands cold

when I might strike a match to dry kindling?
The shape of my kettle's a comfort
when wind shakes the latch on my door.
Yet I stand at the sink, my hands cold.

. . . .

Lullaby

Snow is lying on my roof.
I cannot breathe.
Two tons of snow lie on my roof

heavy as the sea,
the loft of grain,
the desert as it gathers sand,
and I have only two small flames
beside my bed. I hear the sea

when I lie down, the sea
inside my head.
The candles sputter when the wind blows.
Snow falls from the trees

like sacks of grain.
No seed can root in snow.
It cannot breathe.
My roof is like an unplowed field.

Who walks upon it?
Rafters creak
as if a wishbone cracked
and I had wished the sky to fall.

Thaw

Hauling my buckets
up this trail, my heavy
boots sliding on ice,
I have moved as a mule

moves, without joy,
and wondered what mules think
when they drag a wagon home.
We found ours frozen

to death in the pasture and what
did he think as his haunches grew stiff,
empty belly stopped rumbling? I thought
how I too might have simply stood

still and become ice, I was that
tired of lifting cold water.
Today the road's shedding
its ice like a snakeskin,

like my own calloused skin
I will scour this very night,
though the almanac says spring
is six weeks away. It lies,

surely it lies. Such a winter
demands early spring, for my face
is so sad from desiring the sun
and my hair dull as rope in the barn.

I am tired of the sight of me
frozen in glass every morning,
as if the moon waited for stones
I will throw in the water.

Quilt

What I see out the door
is a tree trunk
my arms cannot span
and a trough where the mule drinks.

I see many birds eat the crusts
I have scattered.
I see their wings shiver
like eyelids. I see the trail

disappear downhill,
no sign of you on it,
your dust rising toward me,
the flash of your bridle.

I see my front yard as a jumble
of shapes I have never succeeded in piecing
together. The empty pail. Tracks
over new snow. The rats in the woodpile.

What else can I call it
but *Waiting for Spring*?
That old patchwork. The dead
sleep beneath it forever.

· · · · · · · ·

Lineage

This red hair
I braid while she
sits by the cookstove
amazes her. Where
did she get hair the color
of wildfire, she wants to know,

pulling at strands of it
tangled in boar-bristles.
I say from Sister, God knows
where she is, and before
her my grandmother you
can't remember because
she was dead by the time
you were born, though you hear
her whenever I sing,
every song handed down
from those sleepless nights
she liked to sing through
till she had no time
left for lying awake
in the darkness and talking
to none save herself.
And yet, that night
I sat at her deathbed
expecting pure silence,
she talked until dawn
when at last her voice
failed her. She thumbed out
the candle between us
and lifted her hand
to her hair as if what
blazed a lifetime might still
burn her fingers. Yes,
I keep a cinder of it
in my locket I'll show you
as soon as I'm done telling
how she brought up from
the deep of her bedclothes
that hairbrush you're holding
and whispered, "You
might as well take it."

Diamonds

This, he said, giving the hickory leaf
to me. *Because I am poor.*
And he lifted my hand to his lips,
kissed the fingers that might have worn
gold rings if he had inherited

bottomland, not this
impossible rock where the eagles soared
after the long rains were over. He stood
in the wet grass, his open hands empty,
his pockets turned inside out.

Queen of the Meadow, he teased me
and bowed like a gentleman.
I licked the diamonds off the green
tongue of the leaf, wanting only
that he fill his hands with my hair.

. . . .

Easter

Where my father's house stood
at the edge of the cove is a brown church
the faithful call Bosom of God.
I have come back to sit at the window
where I can see apple trees bud
while the preacher shouts death has no victory.

Everywhere dogwoods are blooming
like white flesh this man claims
is devil's work: woman who tasted
the apple and disobeyed God. But for Christ
we are doomed to the worms waking under
these hills I would rather be climbing

again with my father's goats bleating
so loud I can't hear this man say
I must ask the Lord pardon for what
I've come back to remember—the sun
on my neck as I shook loose my braids
and bent over the washpot. My bare feet

were frisky. If wind made the overalls
dance on the clothesline, then why
shouldn't I? Who's to tell
me I should not have shouted for joy
on this hill? It's the wind I praise God for
today, how it lifted my hair like a veil.

. . . .

FRED CHAPPELL

A Prayer for the Mountains

Let these peaks have happened.

The hawk-haunted knobs and hollers,
The blind coves, blind as meditation, the white
Rock-face, the laurel hells, the terraced pasture ridge
With its broom sedge combed back by wind:
Let these have taken place, let them be place.

And where Rich Fork drops uprushing against
Its tabled stones, let the gray trout
Idle below, its dim plectrum a shadow
That marks the stone's clear shadow.

In the slow glade where sunlight comes through
In circlets and moves from leaf to fallen leaf
Like a tribe of shining bees, let
The milk-flecked fawn lie unseen, unfearing.

Let me lie there too and share the sleep
Of the cool ground's mildest children.

. . . .

My Grandfather Gets Doused

He hedged his final bet.
The old man decided, to get saved
You had to get *all* wet.

An early April Sunday he braved
Cold river and a plague
Of cold Baptist stares. He waved

And nodded. I saw his wounded leg
Wince at the touch
Of icy stream-edge.

Righteous clutch
Of the preacher dragged him farther in.
Maybe now he didn't want it much,

But ringed by mutely sniggering men
And contraltos making moues,
He managed a foolish unaccustomed grin

And plunged to his knees in ooze
And rush of Pigeon River.
What a bad black bruise

Of reputation! Never
In a thousand thousand thousand years
Had Davis or Clark turned hard-believer

Baptist. Weeping wormy tears
His Methodist fathers screamed
In paid-for plots. My uncles' sneers

Rose like spiritual kites. Who dreamed
Heresy lurked in his slick Sibelius-like head?
It was not seemly what he seemed.

Dead,
And grounded like a hog or horsefly, would
Be better than raving Baptist. No one admitted

It, but to be good
Was to be Methodist.
And everybody should.

Man, were they ever pissed!
He'd taken the habit of laying down laws,
So now this exhibitionist

Apostasy didn't sit so well.
And they all felt sneaky-content because
There went *his* ass to hell.

They'd togged him out in white,
And he rose from the water with a look
As naked and contrite

As a fifth-grader caught with a dirty book.
Was he truly saved at last?
Before he could take it back

They said the words fast
And hustled him to dry ground
And shook his hand with ungracious haste.

If his theology was unsound,
At least he had a healthy fear
Of dying. . . . He frowned

When he saw me gaping. A double tear
Bloomed at the rim of his eye.
In a yellow-green willow a finch sang clear

And high.
Silence seized us every one,
Standing bemused and dry.

Now O pitiful he looked. The sun
Cloud-muffled, a cold wind-stir
Brought us to compassion.

They fetched his clothes from the car;
Still expostulating,
The preacher led him to a laurel thicket where

He changed. *And changed again.* Waiting
In numb wonder, we heard his voice go
Grating.

Baptized he was. But now
He decided to be *un*baptized. Pale
Pale the preacher grew;

I thought his heart would fail.
"No, Mr. Davis, no no no." It couldn't be.
Baptism was all or not at all,

Like virginity.
He'd have to stay washed white,
Baptist through eternity.

"Well, that's all right,"
He said. "But I had no notion it *took* so quick."
His voice glared unworldly light.

Grasped his walking stick,
And saddling his armpit on his crutch, he strode,
Dragging the dead foot like a brick.

At the side of the narrow road
He turned to watch the river driving east.
(Was West Fork Pigeon *really* the Blood

Of the Lamb?) A shadow-creased
Scowl huddled his face
When a thought bubbled up like yeast:

The water that saved him was some place
Else now, washing away the sins
Of trout down past McKinnon Trace.

And now he hoisted his stoic limbs
Into the home-bound Ford. "What damn difference
Will it make?" he said. "Sometimes
I think I ain't got a lick of sense."

. . . .

Rimbaud Fire Letter to Jim Applewhite

That decade with Rimbaud I don't regret.
But could not live again. Man, that was *hard.*
Nursing the artificial fevers, wet
With Falstaff beer, I walked the railyard,
Stumbled the moon-streaked tracks, reciting line
After burning line I couldn't understand.
In the long twilight I waited for a sign
The world its symbols would mount at my command.

My folks thought I was crazy, maybe I was.
Drinking behind the garbage back of Maxine's Grill,
I formulated esoteric laws
That nothing ever obeyed, or ever will.
"Les brasiers, pleuvant aux rafales de givre.—Douceurs!"
I must have dreamed those words a hundred times,
But what they meant, or even what they *were,*
I never knew. They glowed in my head like flames.

Four things I knew: Rimbaud was genius pure;
The colors of the vowels and verb tenses;
That civilization was going up in fire;
And how to derange every last one of my senses:
Kind of a handbook on how to be weird and silly.
It might have helped if I had known some French,
But like any other Haywood County hillbilly
The simple thought of the language made me flinch.

So passed my high school years. The senior prom
I missed, and the girls, and all the thrilling sports.

My teachers asked me, "Boy, where you *from?*"
"From deep in a savage forest of unknown words."
The dialogue went downhill after that,
But our positions were clear respectively:
They stood up for health and truth and light,
I stood up for Baudelaire and me.

The subject gets more and more embarrassing.
Should I mention the clumsy shrine I built
In the maple tree behind old Plemmons' spring?
Or how I played the young Artur to the hilt
In beer joints where the acrid farmers drank?
Or how I tried to make my eyes look *through?*
—I'd better not. Enough, that I stayed drunk
For eight hot years, and came up black and blue.

One trouble was that time was running out.
Rimbaud had finished "all that shit" before
He reached his nineteenth year. I had about
Nineteen short months to get down to the core.
I never did, of course. I wrote a bunch
Of junk I'm grateful to have burned; I read
Some books. But my courage was totally out to lunch.
Oh, Fred Fred Fred Fred Fred . . .

Remember when we met our freshman year?
Not something you'd want to repeat, I guess, for still
R. worked his will in me, a blue blear
Smoke poured forth. (That, and alcohol.)
(And an army of cranky opinions about whatever
Topic was brought up.) (And a hateful pose
Of expertise.) Jesus, was I clever!
And smelt myself as smelling like a rose.

I had a wish, "Mourir aux fleuves barbares,"
And to fulfill it could have stayed at home.
But down at Duke in 1954
(*I like Ike*) it carried weight with some

Few wild men and true who wanted to write
And even tried to write—God bless them
Everyone!—and who scheduled the night
For BEER and the explication of a POEM.

Well, you recall: Mayola's Chili House,
Annamaria's Pizza, Maitland's Top Hat,
The Pickwick, and that truly squalid place,
The Duchess, where the local whores stayed fat
On college boys, and the Blue Star, the I.
P.D. But the joint that really made us flip
Sat sunsoaked on Broad St., where we walked by
Rambeau's Barber Shop.

Those were the days! . . . —But they went on and on and on.
The failure I saw myself grew darker and darker.
And hearing the hard new myths from Bob Mirandon,
I got Rimbaud confused with Charlie Parker.
It was a mess, mon vieux. Finally
They kicked me out, and back to the hills I went.
But not before they'd taught me how to see
Myself as halfway halved and halfway blent.

Jim, we talked our heads off. What didn't we say?
We didn't say what it cost our women to prop
Our psyches up, we couldn't admit *the day*
And age belonged still to our fathers. One drop
Distillate of Carolina reality
Might have cured much, but they couldn't make us drink.
We kept on terribly seeing how to see,
We kept on terribly thinking how to think.

They turned me down for the army. I wanted it raw,
I wanted to find a wound my mother could love.
("Il a deux trous rouges au côté droit.")
I wanted Uncle Sugar to call my bluff . . .
No soap. I wound up hauling fertilizer,
Collecting bills, and trying to read Rimbaud

At night, and preaching those poems to David Deas or
Anyone else I thought might care to know.

The only good thing was that I got married.
And I watched the mountains until the mountains touched
My mind and partly tore away my fire-red
Vision of a universe besmirched.
I started my Concordance to Samuel Johnson,
And learned to list a proper footnote, got down
To reading folks like Pope and Bertrand Bronson,
And turned my back on the ashes of Paree-town.

But as my father said, "Fire's in the bloodstream."
The groaning it cost my muse to take off my edge
Still sounds in my sleep, rasps my furious dream.
—Tell you what, Jim: let's grow old and sage;
Let's don't wind up brilliant, young, and dead.
Let's just remember.
                              —Give my love to Jan.
Yours for terror and symbolism,
                                        ole Fred.

28 May 1971

. . . .

My Mother Shoots the Breeze

Hot horn hand in my face is all,
The old days. Not that I'm not glad you honor
Daddy and Mama by remembering.
But it wasn't eggs in clover by any means.
To belong like that to Old Times, you belong
To cruelty and misery . . . Oh.
I can't say just what I mean.

Whenever they talk to *you* they leave out hurting.
That's it, everybody hurt. The barns
Would hurt you, rocks in the field would bite like snakes.
And girls have skinny legs, eaten up

By rocks and briars. But I knew always a man
Was looking for me, there was a man would take me
Out of the bottom cornfield for my soul.
My Mama sent me to Carson-Newman College
And the University of Tennessee.
I came back home a schoolmarm, and could watch
Out my first grade windows women chopping
Tobacco, corn, and rocks in the first spring heat.
Two years before, and that was only me
There chopping, but now the pupils said me Yes Mam.
When I read Chaucer they learned to call me Mam.
I'd go back home and milk the cows and grade
A hundred papers. I'd have milked a thousand cows
And graded papers till my eyes went stone
To hear them call me Yes Mam before my Mama.
I taught how to read and write my first grade class
Of six-year-olds and big farm boys and grandmothers.
I'm not humble I was schoolbook proud.

First time I met your Pa he took my slip
Off. "Miss Davis, I want your pretty slip,
If you've got one loose about, for my Science class."
He was going to fly them Benjamin Franklin's kite.
I went to the women's room and squirmed it down
And sneaked it to him in a paper bag.
Under the table at lunch he grinned like a hound.
That afternoon he patched the kite together
And taught them about Electricity.
"Touch that, boys," he said, "if you want a shock.
We've got Miz Silverside's silk panties here."
(Jake Silverside was our Acting Principal.)

But I knew better what I couldn't say
And giggled like a chicken when that kite
Sailed up past my fifth period Spanish window.
I don't know what to tell you how I mean,
But I felt it was me, seeing my slip
Flying up there. It was a childish folly

But it made me warm. I know there's pictures now
Of people doing anything, whatever
Only a doctor could think of, but my slip,
Scented the way that I alone could know,
Flying past the windows made me warm.
J.T.'s the man I want, I thought, *because
He'd do anything* . . . And so he would.

But wouldn't stop . . . Everyday two weeks
In a row he ran that kite up past my window,
Long after he had worn Ben Franklin out.
It's time to show that man that I mean business,
I thought, it's time we both came down to earth.
The very next day I borrowed my daddy's 12 gauge
And smuggled it to school under a raincoat,
And when that kite came past me one more time
I propped and took my time and lagged and sighted
And blew the fool out of it, both barrels.
It floated up and down in a silky snow
Till there was nothing left. I can still remember
Your Pa's mouth open like the arch of a bridge.
"Quit troubling us maiden girls with your silly Science,"
I said, "while we're learning to talk to Mexico."

And one month later, after we were married,
He still called me Annie Mexico.

So. You're the offspring of a shotgun wedding,
But I don't blush about it much. Something
Your father taught me: *Never apologize,
Never be ashamed, it's only life* . . .
And then he was fired for creating life
From alfalfa in a jar on a window sill.

But look, I've told the story that was fun,
And I didn't mean that. What I meant to tell you:
It was hard, hard, hard, hard,
Hard.

My Father Washes His Hands

I pumped the iron handle and watched the water
Cough his knuckles clean. Still he kept rubbing,
Left hand in his right like hefting a baseball;
The freckles might have scaled off with the clay.
But didn't. They too were clay, he said, that mud
The best part maybe of apparent spirit.

"What spirit?" I asked.
                     He grinned and got the soap
Again and sloshed. A bubble moment I saw
Our two faces little in his palm.
"The Spirit of Farming," he said, "or the Soul of Damnfool."
Our faces went away and showed his lifeline.
"Damnfool why?"
                 "A man's a fool in this age
Of money to turn the soil. Never a dime
To call his own, and wearing himself away
Like a kid's pencil eraser on a math lesson.
I've got a mind to quit these fields and sell
Cheap furniture to poor folks. I've got a mind
Not to die in the traces like poor Honey."
(Our jenny mule had died two weeks before.)
"A man's not the same as a mule," I said.

He said, "You're right. A man doesn't have the heart . . .
We buried Honey, me and Uncle Joe,
While you were away at school. I didn't tell you.
Two feet down we hit pipe clay as blue
And sticky as Buick paint. Octopus-rassling,
Uncle Joe called it. Spade would go down
Maybe two inches with my whole weight behind
And come up empty. Blue glue with a spoon.
I soon decided to scale down the grave.

I told him straight, *I'm going to bust her legs
And fold them under.* His face flashed red at once.

My God, J.T., poor Honey that's worked these fields
For thirteen years, you'd bust her legs? I nodded.
She can't feel a thing, I said. He says,
By God I do. I told him to stand behind
The truck and stop his ears. I busted her legs.
I busted her legs with the mattock, her eyes all open
And watching me crack her bones and bulging out
Farther slightly with every blow. These fields
Were in her eyes, and a picture of me against
The sky blood-raw savage with my mattock.
I leaned and thumbed her eye shut and it was like
Closing a book on an unsatisfactory
Last chapter not pathetic and not tragic,
But angrifying mortifying sad.
The harder down I dug the bluer I got,
And empty as my shovel. It's not in me
To blubber, don't have Uncle Joe's boatload
Of whiskey in my blood yet. Heavy is how
I felt, empty-heavy and blue as poison.
So maybe it's time to quit. The green poison
Of money has leached into the ground
And turned it blue . . . That grave is mighty shallow
That I dug, but I felt so out of heart I couldn't
Make myself go farther and farther down.
I stopped waist-high and we built up a mound
That will soak away by springtime and be level."

"Are you really going to quit the farm?" I asked.
"I wouldn't quit if I could get ahead,
But busting my behind to stay behind
Has got to be the foolishest treadmill a man
Could worsen on. The farm can wait; there's money
To be made these days, and why not me?
Better me than some cheap crooks I know of,
And that's a fact."
                    "Whatever you say," I said,
"It's kind of sad, though . . . And now old Honey's gone."
"*Gone?* Six nights in a row I'd close my eyes

And see her pawing up on her broken legs
Out of that blue mud, her suffering hindquarters
Still swallowed in, and in her eyes the picture
Of me coming toward her with my mattock;
And talking in a woman's pitiful voice:
Don't do it, J.T., you're breaking promises. . . .
And wake up in a sweat. Honey's not gone,
She's in my head for good and all and ever."
"Even if you quit the farm?"
                                   "Even if."

I handed him the towel. He'd washed his hands
For maybe seven minutes by the clock,
But when he gave it back there was his handprint,
Earth-colored, indelible, on the linen.

. . . .

The Story

Once upon a time the farmer's wife
told it to her children while she scrubbed potatoes.
There were wise ravens in it, and a witch
who flew into such a rage she turned to brass.

The story wandered about the countryside until
adopted by the palace waiting maids
who endowed it with three magic golden rings
and a handsome prince named Felix.

Now it had both strength and style and visited
the household of the jolly merchant
where it was seated by the fire and given
a fat gray goose and a comic chambermaid.

One day alas the story got drunk and fell
in with a crowd of dissolute poets.
They drenched it with moonlight and fever and fed it
words from which it never quite recovered.

Then it was old and haggard and disreputable,
carousing late at night with defrocked scholars
and the swaggering sailors in Rattlebone Alley.
That's where the novelists found it.

. . . .

Abandoned Schoolhouse on Long Branch

The final scholar scrawls his long
Black name in aisle dust, licks the air
With his tendril double tongue,
Coils up in shadow of a busted chair

And dozes like the farmer boys
Who never got straight the capital
Of Idaho, found out the joys
Of long division, or learned what all

Those books were all about. Most panes
Are gone now and the web-milky windows
Are open to the world. Gold dust-grains
Swirl up, and show which way the wind blows.

K.B. + R.J., cut deep
In a darkened heart on the cloakroom wall.
Now Katherine Johnson and Roger sleep
Quite past the summons of the morning bell.

The teacher sleeps narrow too, on yonder
Side of Sterling Mountain, as stern
With her grave as with a loutish blunder
In the Bible verse she set them to learn.

Sunset washes the blackboard. Bees
Return to the rich attic nest
Where much is stored. Their vocalese
Entrances the native tranquil dust.

Narcissus and Echo

Shall the water not remember   *Ember*
my hand's slow gesture, tracing above   *of*
its mirror my half-imaginary   *airy*
portrait? My only belonging   *longing;*
is my beauty, which I take   *ache*
away and then return, as love   *of*
teasing playfully the one being   *unbeing.*
whose gratitude I treasure   *Is your*
moves me. I live apart   *heart*
from myself, yet cannot   *not*
live apart. In the water's tone,   *stone?*
that brilliant silence, a flower   *Hour,*
whispers my name with such slight   *light:*
moment, it seems filament of air,   *fare*
the world become cloudswell.   *well.*

. . . .

Teller

The money appears as jittery fireflies
Her black screen has netted. They suspend
A moment within their small abyss,
They tell their little story and go away.
Her computer circumspectly peeps; displays
New constellations of number without end,
Mint-green and cool and dry,
As fleeting and irrevocable as a kiss.

What an ardent gossip it is, this sleek machine!
Nothing but rumors of money the livelong day.
It tells her everything but where the money is,
Or if it really exists. Probably
It doesn't exist. It's only Business,
Something you have to take on faith to mean

Something. A ghost, like PERKINS, P T, whose name
Appears before her in letters of ghostly flame.

But isn't that the truth no one is telling?
The people don't exist, nor even the money.
No one is actually out there, only the box
Throbbing to its mates like a cricket.
That's why she feels so alone. It's funny
She never thought, except it's such a killing
Thought: Everybody lonely
Except the box which would like to feel lonely,
Or happy or bored or nostalgic—or downright wicked.

. . . .

From *C*

VIII   Daisy

> Men build Parises and Zions;
>   I, wide meadows of Orions.
> Rome took two thousand years, but in one day
>   I built a Milky Way.

XIV   First Novel

And then in April the old priest died.
Your mother, the letter said. *Come soon.*
The blonde girl looked at him and sighed.
Over the silent lake the moon.

"I love only you," said the doctor's wife.
They were struggling for the pistol when
He suddenly realized that his life.
It rained in Paris next day again.

xv   Upon a Confessional Poet

You've shown us all in stark undress
The sins you needed to confess.
If my peccadilloes were so small
I never would undress at all.

xxiii   Literary Critic

Blandword died, and now his ghost
Drifts gray through lobby, office, hall.
Some mourn diminished presence; most
Can see no difference at all.

xxiv   Another

Dr. Cheynesaugh has one rule
That makes all others void and null,
Embodying this sentiment:
Guilty till proven innocent.

xxv   Another

Professor Pliant flits from school to school.
An Archetypal Marxian Feminist,
A faithful Structural Deconstructionist,
His beige enthusiasms never cool.

And never warm. As any führer's disciple
He finds himself unable to confute or
Challenge the weakest intellectual cripple.
He is the very model of a hermeneuter.

xxxi Televangelist

He claims that he'll reign equally
With Jesus in eternity.
But it's not like him to be willing
To give a partner equal billing.

liii El Perfecto

Senator No sets up as referee
Of everything we read and think and see.
His justification for such stiff decreeing
Is being born a perfect human being
Without a jot of blemish, taint, or flaw,
The Dixie embodiment of Moral Law,
Quite fit and eager to pursue the quarrel
With God Whose handiwork he finds immoral.

xcix Apology

If any line I've scribbled here
Has caused a politician shame
Or brought a quack a troubled night
Or given a critic a twinge of fear
Or made a poet's fame appear
Transitory as candleflame,
Why then, I gladly sign my name:
Maybe I did something right.

. . . .

WILLIAM HARMON

Mothsong

Some dust,

such as it is,
is transferred from a mother's album
to a son's turning finger,

then from the finger
to the front of a dark coat,
once a father's,

and then, some months later, from there
to the substance found
on a newborn moth's wing,

witnessed intermittently from below
colliding fitfully with the frosted globe
of a simple fixture
in the middle of a kitchen ceiling,

an irregular but redundant disturbance,
turning, stubborn, a tolling
of sorts, or
a knocking,

like something asymmetrical happening,

the song of an old fork
going, going, gone downstairs.

And so from that moth now
back to this paper—not
so far after all
from the heavy black pages
of a mother's mandatory album under a table lamp,

bland perfunctory public paper
here in the hand,
to be balled up,

a fist, a mind,
a clenched white apple
hanging in a darkening orchard.

.   .   .   .

The House

Now the only thing the house has ever really wanted to do is fly, but it is
    unable to.
It has wings, east and west, but they are wings of occidental hardwood
    fastened to lead beams by means of mortal nails.

The fists of Epictetus come punching through the weak ceiling.
Avuncular knees (they look sneaky, like Calvin's in Geneva) insinuate
    themselves through the cracks of vacuum dust.

Spangled shingles shine under the double eagle sun and moon.

Santas violate the flue, detonating the glassware that used to come with the
    purchase of eight or more gallons of regular gasoline.
Superposed on Luther's smooth face's five-o'clock shadow, Philipp
    Melanchthon's blackened eyes and nose come abruptly up out of the
    bathtub, mouthing "ONO."

Again the house tries to lift itself,
But its bones, once light and hollow, have been pumped full of sheetrock
    and steel wool.

Even so, the house tries to lift, as in a dream you try to move out of the way
    of an oncoming bus but cannot.

That is how the earthbound house will wake up suddenly some nights as
though a storm of leaves and feathers were to stir the waves of the world
with long spoons.

. . . .

Redounding

Responsively
Our whole house shakes to the thunder's psalm,

Windows react
To the wind's offices, and I am turned all the way around

By the bold sound
That represents, in one sense, almost nothing at all

But, in another sense,
The presence of an old God—popular,

Avuncular,
Gullible, petty, sports-minded, omnipotent, girl-crazy,

But nothing now
But noise, with some nominal vestiges of awe. One

Could tell it to
Roar on. Byron told (James said "besought") the deep blue sea

To roll,
Longfellow told the flower of the lily to bloom on. Romanticism

Did things
Like that. Redundant. So what the hell: throw

Your hammer, Thor!
Thunder, thunder. Be yourself. Provoke apostrophes. That's it.

Totem-Motet

A really large wristwatch
With its crystal shattered
Complicatedly
In many places,
The Atlantic Ocean
Clicks in its compound cell,
Complaining about feeling
Too cooped up, suffering
Fearsome cramps in the main-
Spring, fragile balance
Wheel, and the detaining catch
Of the delicate escapement.
Cracks in the curved crystal
Crack among themselves, not like pistol
Cracks but like religions
Progressively subdividing
Until each child
Is a church unto herself,
Complaining bitterly
About her lot, her alloted slot,
The spot no household compound
Can lift, unless it be
Plain salt water in a beaker
At sea, tipping impromptu
First one way, then another,
Between peril and peril:
The timing mechanism
Of a complicated schism.

. . . .

Zubby Sutra

(Introduction to a Farewell to Religionswissenschaft)

You know, reading the Bhagavadgita at bedtime can have its drawbacks;
last night, for instance, falling asleep in that ebbing free fall in
wandering mazes of direct or indirect objects lost, I floated undulant

A waffle iron I paid four dollars for
Secondhand, then spent nine dollars to get fixed.

About four minutes at the "Medium" setting.
Allow for some expansion.

The *Joy of Cooking* is a genuine classic.
A nobler book than *Moby-Dick*, and indexed.

Invoice No. 27   He-Who-May-Say

Listen, silent gentles:
There is nothing there.
Mothers, fathers, sisters, brothers, listen.

I have seen the future.
I have been there. Manic-mantic, I have it all by heart.
And I can tell you there is nothing there.

Nothing, nothing. No thing, not one ant or gnat,
Not the least shadow of the merest ash,
No bones about,
No atom, no smallest mote of comic-cosmic dust,
No mite, no item, no iota.
Just blessed blissfulnesses just and just.

Look, O children of all ages of all Ages,
O thrones, worms, wandering idiots lost beyond dogs' orbits,
Wallflowers woefully unbeckoned,
Infatuated sots of mean sobriety,
Superstitious nincompoops, unsound, inane-insane,
O silent gentles, look, look, look at it this way:

If you can say you are awake today,
Or even guess you think you may be, "some,"
Then there you are, right, right there and then,
Right here right now, just that much that,

No matter whether ten or ten-times-ten
Recyclings of the crystal year, whatever sum
(After the first second there is no second:
You're on your own), if
You are here and now
Awake—O vivid invisible center of my homely homily!—
Then it must have to be the case,
It must, that is, befall that you are wholly blessed,
Under the aegis, under the auspices, under something
That has sponsored you and sheltered you forever.

Make no mistake:
You could not let a second's breath
Without the unanimous permission of the one universe.
And you have that. You do.
You have it all the time, all tides, all times,
But never quite so much and perfectly
As when you absolutely least expect it,
Between two bites (say) of a Milky Way.

. . . .

SUSAN LUDVIGSON

Some Notes on Courage

Think of a child who goes out
into the new neighborhood,
cap at an angle, and offers to lend
a baseball glove. He knows
how many traps there are—
his accent or his clothes, the club
already formed.
Think of a pregnant woman
whose first child died—
her history of blood.
Or your friend whose father
locked her in basements, closets,
cars. Now when she speaks
to strangers, she must have
all the windows open.
She forces herself indoors each day,
sheer will makes her climb the stairs.
And love. Imagine it. After all
those years in the circus, that last
bad fall when the net didn't hold.
Think of the ladder to the wire,
spotlights moving as you move,
then how you used to see yourself
balanced on the shiny air.
Think of doing it again.

. . . .

In the Beginning

The day she began to cry, ironing,
I sat in a square of light
on the kitchen floor
learning to print my name.
I remember the *S*
kept coming out backward.

In tears, one hand clenching a shirt,
she bent to draw me a letter,
then forgot me and wept for hours.

As the sun moved higher
my linoleum spot changed shape,
elongated, until
the paper's edge would not fit
to its rim.

I listened, studied,
in shadow, then in dark,
forming that one imperfect word.

. . . .

Jeanne d'Arc

To be chosen—

my small body rejoices
at the words,
encases itself in silver
more lovely than silk.

Not to stay in the village
and marry the miller,
his babies heavy in my arms
as loaves of bread—

not to be God's bride
dressed in the long black robe
I've secretly named a shroud,
needing always to chasten myself
for my shimmering dreams—

but Christ's innocent mistress,
Lily of war!

Still, I can scarcely believe
how each time I speak
the sky brightens.

When the voice first came
from behind the dark trees
I sat for a long time, trembling.
Now my skin
burns, imagining how it will be,
the horse between my thighs,
a thousand men behind me
singing.

. . . .

Mary

*Mary Ricks, the Wisconsin window-smasher, has
put in an appearance at Eau Claire. She was taken
into custody by a policeman as she was about to
wreck a fine plate glass window.*
—February 22, 1894, the *Badger State Banner*

It was *so clean.* Mother used to say,
if you polish one like that
a man might walk through it,
thinking it a clear passage
to the garden, but be surprised
by the crack and the instantaneous
shock of something slicing his shoulder,
his belly, so that the blood
would run from here to Lake Michigan.
Sometimes I stand outside a greenhouse.
Cardinals batter themselves
on the roof, the sides.
Sometimes I find a sparrow
with a broken neck, but never
any blood. Mother was wrong.

Nobody bleeds but me.
I try to wait till after dark
on the main streets,
but when I can't, someone
always comes too soon. Still,
I have plenty of scars,
and in jail they bring bandages,
are usually gentle with wounds.

. . . .

The Widow

A stranger arrives at her door
in a T-shirt, his truck
parked outside like a sign:
This is an honest repairman.
He wants directions, but she
does not know the street.
When he asks to use the phone,
she lets him into the kitchen
where the water has just begun
to boil, steaming the windows
like breath.

She remembers the novel
where a man holds a knife
to a child's small throat,
drawing a thin line of blood,
then takes the young mother
off in his truck to rape her.
She thinks where her knives are,
imagines throwing the water
straight from the stove
in his face.

He murmurs something
into the phone.

She has gone to another room
and can't make out the words,
the tone is too soft,
but she hears the water
boil over, spatter the gleaming
stainless steel of her range
like the hiss of firecrackers
before they explode.
He pulls the pan off the burner,
calls to her,
Lady? Lady?

She hides in the bathroom,
listens, even after she hears
the door open again, and close
like the click of a trigger.
When at last the truck
pulls away, she comes out,
spends the whole afternoon
drifting back and forth
to the window.

Making supper,
she burns her hand,
cries softly
long after the pain is gone.

The next morning, she's amazed
to see she'd forgotten
to lock the back door,
to turn off the lights
that burned all night
in the kitchen.

Man Arrested in Hacking Death Tells Police
He Mistook Mother-in-Law for Raccoon

Every morning she'd smear something brown
over her eyes, already bagged
and dark underneath, as if that would
get her sympathy. She never slept,
she said, but wandered like a phantom
through the yard. I knew it. Knew
how she knelt beneath our bedroom window too,
and listened to Janet and me.

One night when *again* Janet said No,
I called her a cow, said she might as well
be dead for all she was good to me.
The old lady had fur in her head
and in her ears,
at breakfast slipped and told us
she didn't think the cows would die.

Today when I caught her
in the garage at dawn, that dyed hair
growing out in stripes, eyes
like any animal surprised from sleep
or prowling where it shouldn't be,
I did think, for a minute,
she was the raider of the garden,
and the ax felt good, coming down
on a life like that.

. . . .

The Man Who Loves Coal

Summer, a hint of fall,
then Indian summer—
my neighbor shovels coal.

His shed in the little courtyard
is filled to its long tin roof.
What can need to be done
in August, September, October,
when cold has not even put its foot
in the door? By 5:00 A.M. he's out there
shoveling, pouring coal through a chute.

Even the pigeons don't begin cooing
so early. By 7:00 I hear their wings.
But my neighbor gets up long before dawn
to his noisy, unaccountable work.

The woman who owns my apartment
complained to the city last year:
coal dust edges her new beige carpet
the length of the window wall.
The authorities promised action—
he's breaking a code.

Still, day after day I'm wakened
by the man whose mission it is
to worry coal.
His ground-floor apartment
is tiny as mine;
what does it take to warm him?
Does he dream of winters
in Sweden, long enough to need fire
until May, and night enough to absorb him?

What draws a man out of his bed
to break the summery silence
scraping   scraping
a concrete floor,
revising places for coal?

Paris Aubade

Breathing, the last possession
that counts, comes faster here, where
time and our oldest obsessions

make us more conscious—self-conscious. The air
is completely polluted, of course, but haze
that descends on this city is like the fair

skin of Doris Day, filmed in the days
when soft light meant dropping gauze
in front of the camera. It's like that these lazy

first weeks when we stay in bed until noon, lawless
as coupling cats we hear on the balcony, late.
We inhale each morning as if the flawed

fabric of earlier lives had been laid
in a drawer, carefully folded, forever.
Yet under the net of that dream, we pay

for what we know. Bodies that flail under covers
all hours in pleasure learn to count breaths—
just after. Though the world falls away for lovers

as they make the escape into flesh,
its heavy atmosphere fills them. Clouds
are the color of nipples. Worn silk thins to mesh.

.   .   .   .

New Physics

And if we should collide with such force,
might we fly off in different directions
and disappear, leaving, in our place,
some new combination that isn't us, really?

I've always imagined your fear
was something like that, even before
there was a language to explain it. Now
I think I partly understand
your flight, after love, from the room
where we watched through open windows
the stars and their discrete pulsing.

I speak of this, of you, as if we were
still present tense, as if you hadn't
once more approached the rim of my life,
that wobbly circumference, then chosen,
again, a safe trajectory. Once a month,
on schedule, I retrace those paths
as if there were something new I could learn,
some variable I might change,
and the world would be different.

Even these thousands of miles
do not annihilate your pull.
When you are asleep and dreaming,
I turn toward the visible moon, pale
in a daytime sky, and feel myself spinning.

. . . .

Poem to the Ideal Reader

You are the twin my mother
gave away at birth,
suddenly arrived from out west,
Arizona, where you grew up
with horses and novels and Prokofiev,
your foster parents musicians.
While I thought you'd died,
you were listening to violin concertos
and training colts, waiting
for the day I'd flee the snow

and head for a land
of perpetual blossoms. (Even now,
as winter deepens, red and white camellias
bloom out the bedroom window.)
While you studied desert owls
and words, I ranged innocent
and lonely through the world—
to Spain and France and Italy,
to the sad Balkans. Now you are here,
your old Volkswagen piled to its ceiling,
the whole backseat, with books.
I take you for walks on the beach,
where we stop to watch porpoises—
new to us both—our hair tangling
in the wind. Whatever
lines I suggest, you nod,
your face telling me gently
yes or no. I sleep
so much better, you
in the next room, up reading
all night with candles.

.   .   .   .

Lasting

*When the first radio wave music escaped Earth's
ionosphere, it literally did become eternal. Music, in this
century, has been converted from sound into the clarity of
pure light. Radio has superseded the constraints of space.*
—Leonard Shlain, *Art & Physics*

Imagine Vivaldi suddenly falling
on the ears of a woman
somewhere beyond Alpha Centauri,
her planet spun into luminescence
aeons from now. She might be
much like us, meditating

on the body, her lover murmuring
to the underside of her breast
before its heaviness suspends,
for a moment, the lift and pause
of his breath. A music she almost knows
drifts through centuries, startling,
augmenting her pleasure.
When earth is particles of dust,
Orson Welles may still strike fear
into the hearts of millions
who wake one morning, unaware
that light has arrived
as an audible prank. Ezra Pound might rasp
his particular madness from an Italy
still alive in arias that shower
into the open windows
of a world youthful as hope.
When books are no longer even ashes,
and no heart beats in any space
near where we were, suns
may intersect, and some of our voices
blend into choirs, the music of the spheres
adrift among new stars.

. . . .

MICHAEL McFEE

Directions

Come by the fast road as far as the river
    with a funny name. Turn left over
the shoal bridge—it will have been repaired
      since that recurrent nightmare.
Pass the valley school, standard fortress of brick,
      and the transforming power lake.
You will come to one stoplight, local joke, facing
      a mostly vacant volunteer plaza—
fire department, branch library, P.O. Turn right,
        away from the veneer of lights.
When you face a choice at the triple fork, follow
         the leftmost tine, toward that low
mountain; and when you buck across the sunken asphalt
         patch that looks like Africa,
bear left again, just past the weed-cracked gas
         station. After the underpass
the road gets narrow, convoluted—quick climb and fall,
         gravel or trash scattered in all
the worst turns—before it unexpectedly yields
        to countryside. Look for a field
spread to the left, a bungalow pinning its far corner:
      home at last. Park in the yard.
If I'm not on the porch, leave your bags on the lawn,
      come inside and lie down on
the ready bed for a while. If daylight grows lean
      and still I haven't been seen,
go out the back, downslope, to the old logging trail,
      a star-lost lovers' lane. You will
enter a cedar plantation, the steady rumor of creek.
    And the closer to it you get,
the more familiar everything feels, until you know,
    paused on the crossing stone,
that I have been watching you all along.

First Radio

A plastic transistor from Japan,
aqua, with black vinyl straps, some chrome trim,
an ear-sized speaker, dials like nails—
perfect in the pocket as a pack of cigarettes,
its hidden heart pulsing over mine.

At lunch, at recess, on the bus,
each fall I'd strain to crack the glamorous code
of the World Series, pinching bright flags
of foil around the bent antenna,
hoping to attract Mantle or Koufax or Gibson.

And at night, planting it under my pillow
like a tooth, like a magic seed,
I'd fall asleep to top-40 big-city dee-jays
bouncing off cloud cover thousands of miles away,
better than any answered prayer.

. . . .

Bach, Beethoven, Brahms, Mendelssohn, Mozart, Schubert, and Schumann

Seven years in the cramped hot heaven
of the choir loft, for seven statuettes,
an ensemble of immortal shrunken heads
whose music we were never allowed to sing
unless simplified into Baptist hymns.

How I hated the angelic robe, its girlish
skirts and sleeves and bow! How bored I was
staring at the endless backside of sermons,
Mrs. Reynolds omniscient in the sanctuary,
ready to report our least whisper or giggle.

And so I'd daydream, flooding the church
until we could cannonball from the balcony,
exchanging the pews for a parquet court,
converting the pulpit into a concert stage
for the only local appearance by the Beatles.

But I loved those busts, the strange wedge
of their torsos, their fancy jackets and ties,
their long hair and even sideburns or beards,
the fingered relief of their foreign names,
the music in their vacant gazes, dreaming . . .

. . . .

Shooting Baskets at Dusk

He will never be happier than this,
lost in the perfectly thoughtless motion
of shot, rebound, dribble, shot,

his mind removed as the gossipy swallows
that pick and roll, that give and go
down the school chimney like smoke in reverse

as he shoots, rebounds, dribbles, shoots,
the brick wall giving the dribble back
to his body beginning another run

from foul line, corner, left of the key,
the jealous rim guarding its fickle net
as he shoots, rebounds, dribbles, shoots,

absorbed in the rhythm that seems to flow
from his fingertips to the winded sky
and back again to this lonely orbit

of shot, rebound, dribble, shot,
until he is just a shadow and a sound
though the ball still burns in his vanished hands.

Cold Quilt

Our clear-eyed guide said it is the slick
cotton that makes quilts cold. I wonder
if it isn't the enduring dowry of bitterness
stitched into them that makes us shiver,
as in that quilt (unfit for hanging) handed
down to me from my father's mother, begun
the day her husband died, a lifelong lament

composed of old suits and shirts he'd worn,
threaded to her leftover dresses, its design—
each pane a basket of memorial flowers,
a dozen loud triangles tipped on their sides—
a stiff pastiche of grief and the solitary
nights spent trying to transform their bad luck
into something useful, used. No busy bee

touched that quilt. Her life became a patchwork
of quilted plenty, her backyard a dormitory
of vegetable beds, her table a dazzling pattern
of cakes and pies. But she stayed skinny
and wrapped herself in the plain handmade cocoon
of that death-quilt every night, even when
she began to fade in her children's spare beds.

At the funeral home, my uncle the soldier
draped her coffin with it, prayed, then handed
that life's flag to me, compactly folded, her
crooked stitches and nearly-rotten panes still
tenacious after half a century, the sheep
I count now in the inherited dark, her cold quilt
a poultice I spread on my chest before sleep.

Uncle Homer Meets Carl Sandburg

After the nervous young professor read "Grass"
aloud to his G.I.-packed class, then said
that the author now lived only a few counties away,
my mother's renegade brother resolved to speak his thanks
to this poet who piled his lines high with bodies
and understood the need simply to get on with our work.

For almost four years, Uncle Homer's sole work
had been to urge his bad feet across Europe, its grass,
its mud, its rotten roads. *I've seen enough bodies
to last me nine lifetimes* was all he ever said
about it. His dreams flickered with the skeletal thanks
of prisoners whose camps they freed, so far away
from the tranquil Blue Ridge.
                                        And so he found a way
to borrow a friend's new Olds and beg off work
that weekend. The drive was a soldier's belated thanks-
giving, the road orbiting Pisgah, the goat-grass
glowing in the pasture below Sandburg's house. Homer said
I cover all as he parked between the sleeping bodies
of roadside hounds.
                                He tried to imagine the bodies
that could cover this field, the stench drifting away
into the safe hazy mountains. His teacher had said
this mansion was first a rich lowlander's, later to work
as Confederate Treasurer, until money was like grass:
"Sandburg made his fortune on the Lincoln books—thanks
be to irony!—then bought the place."
                                        *Many thanks,
Mr. Sandburg*, practiced Homer, scattering the prize bodies
of the Chikaming herd, his eyes lost in soft grass.
Suddenly, like a grenade, he heard, "Hey! Get away!"

He turned to see Carl Sandburg with a stick. "Your work,
sir—" he began, but the flushed poet charged him. "I said
GET AWAY, you!"

Homer slipped backwards in shit, said
shit and scrambled away, shouting over his shoulder, "Thanks
for 'Grass,' sir! Great poem!" It was difficult work
escaping that goat-faced old shepherd, their bodies
a bad vaudeville gag, but my black-sheep uncle pulled away
at last from that shocking head vanishing into the grass.

Homer said he admired Sandburg for that chase, their bodies'
rhyme a kind of thanks, a grace that wouldn't fade away
like dated work or words raised over weed-choked grass.

. . . .

Sad Girl Sitting on a Running Board

She thinks we'll notice her feet first,
laced into tire-colored brogans,
or the way her hand-me-down stockings
stop in a homely doughnut just below the knee,
or how cheap her crumpled sackdress looks
despite piping at collar and cuff.

But it's the painful focus of her face
that stops us, trapped in its pageboy haircut
like chain mail, the gravity already
eroding her eyes and mouth and shoulders,
the world-weariness of those arms
folded in a half-hearted cross on her chest.

It's that eye-level shadow of a hand
pressed into the dusty car door beside her
like fate waiting in an x-ray film,
rising to the breath-warmed surface of a dream
as if to say *Halt, beware, stay back,*
leaving its oily ghost of touch.

Married Couples on Vacation

My mother oils my father's thighs
but he is sleepy, he has just waxed
his black Buick with the whalebone grill
parked right beside them on the beach.
She watches him nap in the hubcap.

My mother takes my father's picture
on the pier, he and his pal from work
have been deep-sea fishing all afternoon.
They hoist their modest catch for her
to take back to the cottage and clean.

My mother poses her new best friend
on the boardwalk, but she looks worried
and the rail has rusted and the bench
is peeling and that row of dark cars
idles near the horizon like a funeral.

My mother makes snapshots of dolphins,
of hotels and palms and peacocks,
of an empty beach scabbed with seaweed.
"It's not as bad," she writes on the back,
"as this might lead you to believe."

Someone takes matching photographs
of my parents beside a cypress lagoon.
My dad looks away. My mom looks back
as, behind her, a dozen flamingos
all bury their heads in the black water.

Wilder Brain Collection, Cornell University

1.
Chalking the time for a test,
I squint through an odd seam of light
between the slates of blackboard:

a permanent display of brains
in the hall outside this classroom.

2.
They float like pickled cauliflower
in a Scotch-rich brine,

shrunken buttocks
petrified in some remote scholarly bog.

3.
"This collection began over a century ago
as a way for experimental psychologists to study
the relationship of the brain to the mind."

For years, they passed out tasteful bequest forms
at alumni dinners, just after dessert.

4.
If you stare at the brains
like a kid trying to catch a minute hand moving,
eventually you'll see it:

they tremble.

Ever so slightly,
like exquisitely-tuned seismic instruments,
they tremble.

And some of them seem to be sweating.

5.
There's Professor Wilder's brain,
a modest specimen, though one expert notes
"a wealth of convolutional development
in the parietal, occipital, and temporal regions."

And there are the rest of his colleagues,
a regular faculty meeting.

But the real celebrity is the murderer Ruloff,
his brain the second largest ever recorded,
so sickeningly big it barely fits
in the glass skull of his jar.

He too was a schoolteacher.
One day he killed his wife and child.
Later he escaped and wrote a "reputable" paper,
"Methods of the Formation of Language."

Someone finally tracked him down and hanged him
and cracked the huge nut of his head

and brought the meat here, a moral display.

6.
Some of the brain lobes are chipped,
some cracked, their hemispherical symmetry
spoiled.

No surprises on the inside,
no mental geodes, just a smooth cross section
of proverbial gray matter.

And some of the brains are still trapped
in a stubborn membrane, a spidery web,
an almost invisible net.

7.

That's exactly where my mother died,
in a cerebral hemorrhage
between the pia and the dura mater,
a stray vessel there sabotaging the brain.

Did she feel a strange pressure beforehand?
Did she fall into light, or darkness, or nothing,
the cumulus of her neutral brain?

8.

It proved impossible to map
the intricate topography of the brain
and then use those contours to predict
or explain the patterns of a mind

so this collection was discontinued
years ago, the field discredited
as another radical branch of phrenology.
Most of the broken brains were thrown away.

9.

I go back into the classroom,
watch the rows of heads inclined
in a kind of intellectual tropism,
as if their brains were drawn
to the light of the paper.

I think how recently my son
mastered the balance of his head,
how only last week my mother
bent to a bright page of words.

I write the final time on the board.

Backwards through the Baptist Hymnal

for Annie Dillard and Belinda

What glorious fossils from the faulty brain,
impressed by rote in remote sanctuaries
or around more distant campfires: what relics,
hauled protestant into our killing air
to demonstrate the double miracle—*memory*
and *song*: what swarm of cicadas, dormant
for 17 years, rising to plague the equinox
with "Is Your All on the Altar?", "Throw Out
the Lifeline!", "Low in the Grave He Lay,"
"At Calvary," "Blessed Assurance," "He Lives!"

From the least scrap, whole hymns accumulate,
words, melodic skeletons, ghostly descants.
B. plies the organ with its comic stops,
Annie gravely brays the melody, while I go
fishing for that plain bass line, surfacing
during refrains to croak, "send the light,"
"I surrender all," "it is well," "by and by."
We backslide through the low-church standards,
proclaiming an unreformed text: plenty of sin
and saving blood, no hootenanny gospel yet.

This may seem a joke to late-chore neighbors,
to God, even to us when I accidentally mash
the swing key when the roll is called up yonder.
It may be an offense against honest silence.
But what could possibly be better than writing
something to be read and sung until finally
anonymous, licked smooth by the flock, something
turned to so often the page is finger-stained,
something, however flawed, that may one night
suddenly come to other tongues as praise?

. . . .

ℋEATHER ℛOSS ℳILLER

Breadstuff

I've had enough of making bread go around,
slapping it, pat-a-caking me to death. But.
Nowhere do I find me so painstakingly
real and rising, leavening each hour
but in this salt, yeast, and cool unblanched flour.
Over the dough bowl, my loony face sifts,
takes shape and lifts. My thumbs search
the elements and my fist blends
the taste of a real presence.
I'd like to waste it, starve people,
go to bed and sleep a year. But.
The oven heats up right
and I wait wait wait.
Crumbs and little bones, sweet dark-curling peels
pile my table, seal the plates. I set out more,
pour cups, catch fish, rob bees to fill up
hungrier, hungrier brothers, nursing all these
on my one lovely body. Never enough.
I make myself go around. Starting over,
I measure and stir, punch the blind stuff
to make it grow. Somebody's tears fall in,
teasing the helpless dough.
Stop it, brothers.
I've got life up to the elbow.

.   .   .   .

Total Eclipse

The Saturday of the eclipse
we woke up crazy and stayed crazy,
feeling the temperature drop ten degrees
and Bear Swamp, in the path of totality,
go dark around 1:29.
The turkey oaks, the sixty-foot pines,

swelled in one great rushing wind,
lifted one green wave.
I stood in the yard shivering,
my arms damp, and thought God God.

Even the security light came on,
the dog barking in circles, crying
over the children. Then he quieted,
his big leery yellow eyes watching us.
Somewhere Pacific the thing started,
south of the equator, traveled Mexico,
the Gulf, over Florida, 1,500 miles per hour
to Bear Swamp. We stood under
a clear black sky and watched
three minutes of fire fight the assault.
I had to respect it.
The cruel sickle-moons dancing,
the hot little fingernails hooking
black pieces out of the sun.
Then long shadow bands started to run
light/dark, eerie as boas on the ground.

For three minutes.
I broke out in goose bumps,
wouldn't look. Our daughter,
hugging closer, kept quiet,
her face remote as the moon.
Our son ran back in the house,
crying like the dog cried, turning
on lights, calling us inside—
two children, like sacrifices,
candles lit at shrines, goldfish thrashing.

Then it was gone.
The sun heaved free and all the roosters
crowed across the highway, the dog sneezing,
jumped to lick our hands, and the eerie boa bands
ran in straight lines off the edge of the world.

The next time we are called
to eyewitness and survive such darkness,
I will be eighty-four, if alive,
the two children sixty, the dog,
Bear Swamp, and you, eclipsed.

.   .   .   .

Gone to Ground

I woke up plain and unadorned
and you were calling to me. I loved
your voice in my name, soft
syllables fleshing the bone, yet dreaded
the undertone my name made
with you inside it.
Your old fleshed-out bony dream
took me by the throat and shook.

But you came on through the dream,
the bellowing morning cows
like a bee swarm behind you. And I sat up
hoping the dream was a good dream,
hoping I got up from bed with you
and when I looked we would be here again,
warm and rich as milk the cows made,
strong as bees, and rising fresh as bread.

I spelled, fingernail to fingernail,
Come back right now quick,
over the Cape Fear River past the park gate.
I'll wait here, quick! I was so sick of life
and I wanted something to give you
to make you stay. Our Eagle Scout son?
Our garlanded May Bride girl?
My peace of mind,
the peace of a tough woman
folded over and gone to ground,
demanded some kind of gift.

The cows and the bees, the slurring river,
lifted and freshened, made themselves up
winged and furred flesh, bone-hard dumb.
You are gone to ground, love,
and my name sticks in your mouth.

. . . .

Twila Jo and the Wrestler

Twila Jo wanted to run off
with a Myrtle Beach wrestler,
tattoos on both his arms,
snaky green things with bicep eyelids
he raised and shut,
wonderful things, things she kissed.
She told her little sister Faye,
the one who saved strings,
the one who crunched foil into big luminous coils
and picked up cans along Ocean Hiway.
"You know better than that,"
the little sister smashed three Pepsis flat,
unraveled a long blue string
from Twila Jo's jeans.
"Look at the mess you already made
sneaking around, and you lied to Daddy."
Little Faye hissed betrayal.
Twila Jo, stark, discordant, brutal,
said, "Daddy can die and so can you"
and drove off to meet the wrestler.

Faye fingered her blue string,
sacked up her three dead Pepsis,
and squatted pinching bright blisters in her foil.
She guessed Twila Jo halfway to Myrtle Beach,
somewhere along Ocean Hiway,
the stupid wrestler reaching across the seat,
flexing the snaky green things,

making Twila Jo squeal and let go the wheel,
then a blue semi, FAYE'S EXPRESS,
flashy as foil, flattening them both
to a bloody blister,
the Myrtle Beach wrestler
and her big sister.

. . . .

Leda Talks

For the first thing:
It was statutory rape.
Under age, cute as a kewpie,
and dumb enough then
to take that Clove chewing gum,
I have since learned some things.
I will get you back. I will stuff you,
stand you against the wall,
and open a Tote-Em-In-Zoo.
The public will walk around, look at you,
your duckfeet and your longhorns,
your feathered glory, your shower of U.S. gold.
They will ask: Where's the hole
to put the nickel in nickel in nickel in?
Say it three times and it comes true.

For the second thing:
You fixed it so I would be well off,
marrying money, living in a high-rise,
and I appreciate it, I really do.
The good husband and I lie glued together all night
and breathe one long black air-conditioned lung.
You got us kids made in Japan:
two older girls, a set of little boy twins.
They sing like angels, take first place
in White Gloves and Party Manners,
play the clarinet, drink and wet.

For the third and final thing:
I aim to throw these kids away
and get new kids like the ones next door,
plain ones, all my own,
who do nothing.
Then my plain kids, my good husband,
and I drive to the Tote-Em-In-Zoo,
put the nickel in and watch you,
old brute, move and mouth
and transmute love.
The detectives in hats and raincoats
show up, "Where's Uncle God?"
I point, "Put your nickel in."
My new kids in white party gloves
kick the machine, "He's a duck, a steer,
the U.S. Mint!"

It is no accident,
they are intelligent.

. . . .

Young Woman in the Shoe

Hours of babies gaudy as pandas
tumble, swell to rhinos, cuddle up
and explode in a rage of little bats
scrambling the rented floor, the green
formica table: her worst dream,
each baby face mews at her,
each fist hooks a bit of skirt
between thumb and wet finger
as she stirs their quick Quaker grits.
She ought to feed them, she ought to.

Before she spreads the table,
the babies spill it, track up her floor
with white desperate paws.

One thing too much hanging on her,
and him, *him!*
her irresistible *him!*
barreling down the sunny interstate,
phoning from the easy truck stops,
Hey, Babe! Whatcha doin, Suge?
So she hits, first them,
then herself, brings the blood,
divides the grits, and ministers
to their enraging and pitiful hunger.
She ought to.

Now bigger bats stud her roof,
pungent as black cloves,
and giant pandas stuff the corner,
while in the bathtub, baby-pink rhinos submerge
to their eyeballs, waiting, *everything dead!*
she did it she did it! her worst dream,
and down the interstate the irresistible
and sunny man returns.

．　．　．　．　．　．　．

In the Natural Course of Things

The day a pony he tried to ride
slung my brother under the Buick,
he bled red across the black asphalt
and I ran upstairs to tell my mother
who said she had a sick headache
and go call the goddamn Rescue Squad.

They sirened over and took a look
at my brother and his blood, said,
How come you let a pony sling you
under a Buick? He said, I don't know,
shut up. And dabbed a finger
in his own blood, staring at it
like it might explain.

In Head Start,
my brother couldn't leave little girls'
long blond hair alone, kept reaching
reaching reaching after something
in their long blond hair not he,
not anybody,
not even they,
could name. He plunged his fingers in,
the little girls shrilled, he pulled
his fingers back
to stare, then willed himself
in their hair all blond again
again again.

After the Rescue Squad
took my brother to an emergency room,
I stood looking at his blood
still bleeding red across the black asphalt.
Shut up, it said. Stick in your finger,
give it a blond name, pull again
again again.

. . . .

In Danger

Next to my mother's zinnia bed,
a fat old man, bald as a snail,
B.V.D.'d and barefoot,
stuffs a wicker chair.
Its dull brown flange flares around him
so that he looks like a dead petunia
or a baby giant,
and his Fatima cigar glows bright as zinnias,
the little red eyes of a tropical bird.
I am in danger.
He puts the cigar to my arm
and it burns like a little biting snake.
He hates me, whispers, "Whatcha say?"

I am nine years old, back home in Badin,
with a good tan and all expressions of shame.
The little biting snake
burns me to death, hurts like a kick
or a joke. I am in danger.
He knows my name.

. . . .

Tap Water

My father wants the water tested.
He thinks it makes my mother crazy,
minerals and poisons, something seeping
off the land, something creeping up on her
when she sips that morning cup, something
making her stare. "Are you that man
who took me to the beach? Did we have
any children?"

Like things flammable and fatal
to swallow, like fortune-telling,
tap water scares the hell out of him,
but he's got to know, got to drink and find out
where she goes at night, what perpetual demons
follow.

The people in white suits collect vials,
one from the yard, another from the kitchen,
they fill out forms my father signs
and they drive off. He blinks
at the puddles in the sink.
My mother polishes her small hands,
one over the other, one over the other,
some compulsive braiding,
some intense and clinging puzzle,
one over the other,
one over the other, one—

I want to interrupt that desperate water,
drop things in and shake the vials, watch the clear
cloud back the green, the virulent blue,
distill my father back my mother,
a familiar strong
uninjured girl.

. . . .

Loss of Memory

Things were going to come out of her mind someday.
Big loud things. And soft ones. Ones smelling
like honeysuckle bright in the shade, sweet,
strangling.

Things were going to take hold.
The soft blond hair of her children,
her face in their hair, her mind swelling,
the taste of salt. She would remember
her children. She would remember
the honeysuckle. She would remember
the big loud things, letters of some alphabet
and bright obnoxious multiplication tables, *and*!
the voices of her own mind shouting back at her
A B C D! Then the blond,
the soft strangle,
the unsayable sweet tangle
of her mind.

. . . .

Delight

Meat eaters,
you believed in meat eaters: Venus fly-traps,
sundews, and pitchers—the rich way they spread their legs,
opened their lips spangled in peril

and licked the struggling bugs—
the way they strangled
everything. You believed, feeling
short hair rise on your neck and love rush
your skin, it was a gift.
But when you tried to lift them from the fragile Carolina bogs,
they resisted like women,
closing their little bitter traps,
leaving sick little drops
on your hand, tight shut, blackening
the dry garden.

What did it take, you raged,
to make these things live with you,
lie down and love you
tenderly tenderly
tongue to tongue
so sweet and so murderous?

The other women from the garden,
common blossoms greedy for sun and air,
spangled the dry hillsides,
and like escaped crazed things,
ate up a world.

.   .   .   .

Cloudless Sulfur, Swallowtail, Great Spangled Fritillary

Out of willows and milkweed and woods around water,
tight tangled places, came her husband's body count.
His atrocities spotted as dice, perfect specimens,
black pansy faces, purple and cream, plain sulfur,
checkerboards, some females
with powdery fringes and starred wings,
they lay under glass in her husband's room,
where she never went if she could help,
except to pull down windows in a rain.

Brutalities pleased him,
these antennae feeble as her own eyelash,
his willful treasures, his dried perfection.
She breathed on the butterflies,
and her breath flexed, then shriveled,
pungent as blue Windex
she sprayed on his mirror. Later,
she slept in the den, forgetting him,
fortunes and blood spattering the TV screen.
Spring Azures tormented her dreams, the tangled array
of Swallowtails, zebra and tiger, black white,
white yellow, blue black blue, pieces
of purple Mourning Cloaks.
Barbarous screams.
His screams.

She woke, face pressed like a waffle, blinking,
her breath no breath, caught in a net, the stinging
unrelenting ether filling up all the space
beyond the moon, between the stars, the upper
upper regions, volatile, colorless, and highly
flammable. A terrible struggle for air.

. . . .

Target

They slip a black silk blindfold over my eyes.
Rifles snap into place and ten men aim
at the little *x*
in the middle of me.
It takes ten, or six, or one,
the smallest military
tactical unit detailed to disperse the bullet.
These people are going to shoot me to death.

The whole world's been gunning for me all night,
so I wonder, sweat feeling its way down my leg,

around around around my neck, I wonder
when I'll turn over to wake up,
the tame friendly sag of the bedsprings
displace these assassins,
the coffee machine blink on, my shower pound
reassuringly the mildewed grout
to deliver me out of this.

Somebody walks up, hands me a king-size cigarette
and a match, one last smoke,
then they tie your hands. I know how it goes.
I inhale, eat the smoke's bitter breath.

These people are going to shoot me to death.

. . . .

Full Color

In your own room, your first room,
the pithy beaverboards skinned in creamy paint
named *Fire Glow, Silhouette, Shadow,*
and *Adoration*, their nailheads like navels
kept something out, you didn't know what,
except your mother, especially.
Your pale room at 86 Spruce, the glass kidney
under the mild mirror and the little pink fuzz of rug
thrown to the floor by the bed, cuddled you,
but the bed your mother saw in *Better Homes & Gardens,*
her own magazine bed, perfect and bewildered,
was a danger bed, devouring bed,
bed prayed in, then escaped.

In your next rooms, your weddings
and babies, the rooms with men,
perfect and bewildered and withstood,
more dangerous and devouring,
you kept something in for good.

Finally your own room again, old,
personal as a fingerprint, whorls
and hangnails intact.

Now you fashion your last room,
the chambered beating thing,
muscular as a boy, into some desperate
loving invincible lie, *Crushed Spice,*
Sweet Butter, Blush, and *Gossamer*—
half-believing, you lean out
to dry your hair in a coloring sun
that hurries the magazine prince,
the darling swindler,
up your fragrant stair.

. . . .

Good Things

Years go by and good things don't happen.
Like people lost somewhere
between the back door
and the car, gone out into the eider drifts,
just stepped out a minute
in all those breast feathers,
and sinking down, never found,
like those imperfect and quick-frozen people,
I keep goosing my way around.
I'm not lost.
I kept this house for years
looking at you, at crumbs stuck in the cracks,
cobwebs cauling the corners, at our attack
of healthy accomplished children,
the ones with loud obnoxious toys,
green chemistry sets and rockets.

Snowed under all night,
our Christmas trees melted loops

of piquant candy lights, peppermint,
tangerine, turquoise.
I wanted you to come get me,
come plunging through the dark, sowing good things
like seed everywhere, a modern Santa Claus,
taking your martini up and with a twist.

Finally,
I just found the car,
a familiar blind lump in the snow,
the imperfect and irresistible car.

You know I want to hurt
something,
and leave a scar.

. . . .

ROBERT MORGAN

Mountain Bride

They say Revis found a flatrock
on the ridge just
perfect for a natural hearth,
and built his cabin with a stick

and clay chimney right over it.
On their wedding night he lit
the fireplace to dry away the mountain
chill of late spring, and flung on

applewood to dye
the room with molten color while
he and Martha that was a Parrish
warmed the sheets between the tick

stuffed with leaves and its feather
cover. Under that wide hearth
a nest of rattlers,
they'll knot a hundred together,

had wintered and were coming awake.
The warming rock
flushed them out early.
It was she

who wakened to their singing near
the embers and roused him to go look.
Before he reached the fire
more than a dozen struck

and he died yelling her to stay
on the big four-poster.
Her uncle coming up the hollow
with a gift bearham two days later

found her shivering there
marooned above a pool
of hungry snakes,
and the body beginning to swell.

. . . .

Face

The story went that once someone, an unbeliever,
looking into the clouds saw among the luminous
caravan of shapes and smokes, the usual sheep

and outcroppings of battlevapor, signals, choo-
choos, stretching fish, when suddenly in
one great chunk of the sky the Lamb himself,

the face of longhaired Jesus, looked sadly down
at him. Struck down on his way from that moment
he believed. Having a camera he snapped the

quickly dissolving icon. Advertised on radio
and at revivals that photo sold thousands. Looking
at the black and white you never found the image

at first, but when it came rushing out of the
wisps and puffs hardening into a perfect likeness
the recognition was beyond all expectation chilling.

For months I kept eyes ahead or to the ground out
of horror, feared looking back I would see
the Tiger clawing through eastern azure.

Double Springs

I used to wonder how
two springs could issue from the hill
a yard apart. Why not dig deeper
and unite their flow?

And later realized they
surfaced close from opposite
directions. The southern
sweeter, though the northern's steady

effluence came cold, even in the dry
months when its neighbor
slacked and almost stood, with
algae thickening the edges.

In the church nearby I've heard
sermons on the trinity describe
their separate currents merging to
one branch. The sweet uneven

head rose from the hillside leaning toward
Dark Corner, while the constant
icy thread emerged
from the farm country. In summer

they condemned the slow one and
when I came down to drink before
or after preaching its partner sure
enough ran clear, with ebullition

dimpling the surface above the pores,
and purifying lizards gripped
the sandy floor. But after swilling
there I'd dip the gourd

into the slightly silty left
embellished now with leaves and spiders
and aquatic mosses for a richer sip.
That ungodly taste I'd carry home.

. . . .

Bricking the Church

At the foot of Meetinghouse Hill
where once the white chapel
pointed among junipers and pulled
a wash of gravestones west,

they've buried the wooden snow that
answered sarvis in bloom
and early morning fogs, in brick,
a crust the same dull red

as clay in nearby gullies.
The little churchhouse now looks more
like a post office or school.
It's hard to find

among the brown winter slopes
or plowed fields of spring.
Brick was prestigious back when
they set their minds and savings to it.

They wanted to assert its form
and presence if not in stone
at least in hardened earth, urban weight,
as the white clapboards replaced

unpainted lumber which replaced
the logs of the original
where men brought their guns to preaching
and wolves answered the preacher.

The structure grows successive rings,
and as its doctrine softens
puts on a hard shell
for weathering this world.

. . . .

Earache

The red wind in my ear would not lay.
I listened through the tunnel of pain
as they carried me pacing the hallway

and in the room where the fireplace ran
cold air. The close ceiling smothered me.
The rose syrup they poured in hurt more than

the night chill. The house throbbed harshly
to the beat behind my eyes, night after night
all winter, till they called a group finally

and chain-prayed in a circle, saying hot
words over my head, each kneeling in turn.
The ache shrank down its nerve and was quiet.

The air stretched cool as whispering vines,
revealing its shifty musics and designs.

. . . .

Blackberries

Among the bloodfilled eyes
and towering vegetation,
invisible
traffic of chiggers.
Leaves bear ticks like hungry berries.
You dive in trampling mole runs

and spilling birdnests,
brush the fanged stems
to gather a few
with the blue jays and yellowjackets.
Wade into the snaky weeds as into a minefield.
Leaves have caught in the briars
and piled up a hive for rats
and spiders.
Quail leave in a snort.
The arching long-necked thickets
weigh with loads of shot
bright as caviar.

.   .   .   .

Lightning Bug

Carat of the first radiance,
you navigate like a creature
of the deep. I wish I could read
your morse across the night yard.
Your body is a piece of star
but your head is obscure. What small
photography! What instrument
panel is on? You are winnowed
through the hanging gardens of night.
Your noctilucent syllables
sing in the millennium of
the southern night with star-talking
dew, like the thinker sending nous
into the outerstillness from
the edge of the orchard country.

Radio

In the corner farthest from the fire,
a safe of carved oak,
cabinet of voices.
The gothic windows stretched with cloth
hide a powerful hum when Grandpa
rolls the knob and the numbers
light up as the needle
passes in its window.
He hunts for the combination.
Birds back somewhere among
the preachers, static, whine
and whistle late at night from forests.
I want to reach in there
and find the jars that sing,
and watch through a gap in the back
the vials glowing in the muck of wires,
a throbbing in the metal
where the languages of the air
are trapped and spoken.
That space unreachable in the small light,
poisoned by electricity.

. . . .

White Autumn

She had always loved to read, even
in childhood during the Confederate War,
and built the habit later of staying up
by the oil lamp near the fireplace after
husband and children slept, the scrub-work done.
She fed the addiction in the hard years
of Reconstruction and even after
her husband died and she was forced
to provide and be sole foreman of the place.
While her only son fought in France

it was this second life, by the open window
in warm months when the pines on the hill
seemed to talk to the creek, or katydids
lined-out their hymns in the trees beyond the barn,
or by the familiar of fire in winter,
that sustained her. She and her daughters
later forgot the time, the exact date,
if there was such a day, she made her decision.
But after the children could cook
and garden and milk and bring in a little
by housecleaning for the rich in Flat Rock,
and the son returned from overseas
wounded but still able and married a war widow,
and when she had found just the right chair,
a rocker joined by a man over on Willow
from rubbed hickory, with cane seat and back,
and arms wide enough to rest her everlasting cup
of coffee on, or a heavy book,
she knew she had come to her place and would stay.
And from that day, if it was one time and not
a gradual recognition, she never crossed a threshold
or ventured from that special seat of rightness,
of presence and pleasure, except to be helped to bed
in the hours before dawn for a little nap.
That chair—every Christmas someone gave her a bright
cushion to break in—was the site on which she bathed
in a warm river of books and black coffee,
varieties of candy and cakes kept in a low cupboard
at hand. The cats passed through her lap and legs
and through the rungs of her seat. The tons
of firewood came in cold and left as light, smoke, ash.
She rode that upright cradle to sleep
and through many long visits with tiers of family,
kissing the babies like different kinds of fruit.
Always hiding the clay pipe in her cabinet
when company appeared. She chaired decisions
to keep the land and refused welfare.
On that creaking throne she ruled a tiny kingdom

through war, death of kin. Even on the night she did
stop breathing, near a hundred, no one knew
exactly when, but found the lamp still on,
the romance open to a new chapter,
and the sun just appearing at her elbow.

. . . .

The Gift of Tongues

The whole church got hot and vivid
with the rush of unhuman chatter
above the congregation,
and I saw my father looking at
the altar as though electrocuted.
It was a voice I'd never heard
but knew as from other centuries.
It was the voice of awful fire.
"What's he saying?" Ronald hissed
and jabbed my arm. "Probably Hebrew."
The preacher called out another
hymn, and the glissade came again,
high syllables not from my father's
lips but elsewhere, the flare of
higher language, sentences of light.
And we sang and sang again, but
no one rose as if from sleep to
be interpreter, explain the writing
on the air that still shone there like
blindness. None volunteered a gloss
or translation or receiver
of the message. My hands hurt
when pulled from the pew's varnish
they'd gripped and sweated so. Later,
standing under the high and plain-
sung pines on the mountain I clenched
my jaws like pliers, holding in
and savoring the gift of silence.

Chant Royal

Born in a notch of the high mountains where
a spring ran from under the porch, on
the second of April just one hundred years
ago this month, my grandpa was a weak one
to start with, premature, weighed a scant
two pounds twelve ounces. So fragile the aunt
who tended that first night feared to move
him except for feeding and the placing of
diapers. He slept near the fire in a shoebox
with one end cut out. Against the odds he would prove
adequate for survival, withstanding all knocks.

Because he was puny his mother would rear
him sheltered, keep him beside her out of the sun
and rain alike, feed him molasses and sulfur in fear
of worms and would let him walk, not run,
to the gap with the others to stand on the slant
bars while the cows were milked in elegant
twilight. Pious and hard, she showed her love
through strictness and was known to reprove
him for the least resistance. She tried raw fox
grape juice and teas of the yarb grannies, strove,
adequate for survival, withstanding all knocks,

to find faith healers, quacks, to cure
her youngest. A cousin wrote of Dr. Wilson
down near Greenville. They took the wagon one clear
morning and reached the town just as the moon
rose full. The man at the door said, "I can't
see you this late," but examined and began to rant
on the virtues of tobacco ("Give him a chew"), then shove
and shoo them out. That night they drove
all the way back. No telling what unlocks
vitality: from that day he began to grow and rove
adequate for survival, withstanding all knocks.

Frampold as any mountain branch, he hunted bees and deer
carried to mill on Cold Friday and learned the fun
of shivarees and drinking. Saw his father appear
walking through the pasture toward him and beckon,
then vanish when he spoke like any haint,
and die within the month. He heard a panther
scream and follow as he came back through the cove
from hogkilling, and sat up nights by the stove
while his brother crisised with the fever and tried to mock
death before it cooled him. Nobody who saw the dove
was adequate for survival, withstanding all knocks.

Out sanghunting he met Mrs. Capps and her
daughter sawing crosscut. The girl could stun
with her beauty, hiding bare feet under leaves. Inner
currents stirred. He quit drinking, came to church, and won
her after three weeks' courting. But they lived in want
the first year; a child died. He made his covenant
one cold night in the orchard and a trove
came in acres for sale cheap on the creek above
the Andrews place. There he sank a well through rock,
weathered debt, depression, set groves,
adequate for survival, withstanding all knocks.

Envoi

Guardian ghost, inhere herein. Before Jove
may this music honor his example, improve
my time as he invested his, and no less unorthodox
discover significance in the bonds his fate wove
adequate for survival, withstanding all knocks.

· · · · · · · ·

Sigodlin

When old carpenters would talk of buildings
out of plumb or out of square, they always
said they were sigodlin, as though anti-

sigodlin meant upright and square, at proper
angles as a structure should be, true to
spirit level, plumb line, erect and sure
from the very center of the earth, firm
and joined solid, orthogonal and right,
no sloping or queasy joints, no slouching
rafters or sills. Those men made as they were:
the heavy joists and studs yoked perfectly,
and showing the dimensions themselves, each
mated pair of timbers to embody
and enact the crossing of space in its
real extensions, the vertical to be
the virtual path of gravity, horizontal
aligned with the surface of the planet at
its local tangent. And what they fitted
and nailed or mortised into place, downright
and upstanding, straight up and down and flat
as water, established the coordinates
forever of their place in creation's
fabric, in a word learned perhaps from
masons who heard it in masonic rites
drawn from ancient rosicrucians who
had the term from the Greek mysteries'
love of geometry's power to say,
while everything in the real may lean just
the slightest bit sigodlin or oblique,
the power whose center is everywhere.

·   ·   ·   ·   ·   ·   ·   ·

Audubon's Flute

Audubon in the summer woods
by the afternoon river sips
his flute, his fingers swimming on
the silver as silver notes pour

by the afternoon river, sips
and fills the mosquito-note air
with silver as silver notes pour
two hundred miles from any wall.

And fills the mosquito-note air
as deer and herons pause, listen,
two hundred miles from any wall,
and sunset plays the stops of river.

As deer and herons pause, listen,
the silver pipe sings on his tongue
and sunset plays the stops of river,
his breath modeling a melody

the silver pipe sings on his tongue,
coloring the trees and canebrakes,
his breath modeling a melody
over calamus and brush country,

coloring the trees and canebrakes
to the horizon and beyond,
over calamus and brush country
where the whitest moon is rising

to the horizon and beyond
his flute, his fingers swimming on
where the whitest moon is rising.
Audubon in the summer woods.

. . . .

Dead Dog on the Highway

Looks already part of the shoulder
mess, assimilated into weeds and tire-peels,
ditch trash. Swollen tight and gray
with diesel grime before we find him,

who loved to fanfare every truck on the dirt road
below the house but had no way to judge
the speed of oncoming playmates
on the wide-lane. The transfer
must have seemed to break from its future
at him. The brake skids show
how far the rig's momentum slapped him
in the last and longest leap of a life
of running cars and fieldmice. Someone
has burst a Falstaff bottle
so he wears a halo of crushed ice.
He looks frozen in mid-gallop except
for the wrongness of the broken back.
The paw pads you want to caress
they're so familiar. A fang exposed
through the sooty underlip bites turf.
Traffic shivers the dirty fur and ear tip.
No blood shows, though ants are busy with the eyes.
The body is so heavy we feel it
must be glued to the dirt as we drag
it to the hole in the embankment,
as though dead flesh having found its bed
would stay there until it soaks
into the topsoil and rots a fume
across the hunting weather.

. . . .

Odometer

We glance always at this little
window of the slowest slot machine
to calendar our progress out.
The meter not ticking is active
just the same, summing up distance
toward the big question, the rollers
marking off ground and still counting.
We're happy no matter how far

gone, to be clocking off the miles,
to keep on breaking our own record
of progress, to make the old wreck
go another revolution
of the thousand wheel, and the ten,
as one candy-size roll of our
numbers turns up another ten times
slower until they all turn up,
in the ode to travel, zero
zero zero zero zero
as it was in the beginning.

. . . .

Rearview Mirror

This little pool in the air is
not a spring but sink into which
trees and highway, bank and fields are
sipped away to minuteness. All
split on the present then merge in
stretched perspective, radiant in
reverse, the wide world guttering
back to one lit point, as our way
weeps away to the horizon
in this eye where the past flies ahead.

. . . .

Vietnam War Memorial

What we see first seems a shadow
or a retaining wall in the park,
like half a giant pool or half
an exposed foundation. The names
start a few to the column at
the shallow ends and grow panel
by deeper panel as though month

by month to the point of opposing
planes. From that pit you can't see much
official Washington, just sky
and trees and names and people on
the Mall and the Capitol like
a fancy urn. For this is a wedge
into the earth, a ramp of names
driven into the nation's green,
a black mirror of names many
as the text of a book published
in stone, beginning almost
imperceptibly in the lawn
on one side and growing on black
pages bigger than any reader
(as you look for your own name in
each chapter) and then thin away
like a ledger into turf again,
with no beginning, no end. As though
the black wall uncovered here a few
rods for sunlight and recognition
runs on and on through the ground in
both directions, with all our names
on the hidden panels, while
these names shine in the open noon.

. . . .

Writing Spider

When Uncle Wass had found the spider's
W woven between the limbs
of a dead chestnut over on
the Squirrel Hill, he said he knew
there would be war. But even before
Pearl Harbor he was gone himself
and my Grandpa, his brother, told
how the writing spider's runes could spell

a message to the world, or warn
of the individual reader's own
end with an initial. That web
was strung significant as lines
in a palm and the little webster,
spinning out its monogram like
the fates, put the whole dictionary
of a life in one elaborate
letter to be abstracted from
the Jacob's ladder of floss and dew
in the eye of the beholder,
a lifetime's work for it and all.

. . . .

Mountain Graveyard

stone   notes

slate   tales

sacred   cedars

heart   earth

asleep   please

hated   death

. . . .

Heaven

And yet I don't want not to believe in,
little as I can, the big whoosh of souls
upward at the Rapture, when clay and ocean,
dust and pit, yield up their dead, when all

elements reassemble into the forms
of the living from the eight winds and flung
petals of the compass. And I won't assume,
much as I've known it certain all along,

that I'll never see Grandma again, nor
Uncle Vol with his fabulations,
nor see Uncle Robert plain with no scar
from earth and the bomber explosions.

I don't want to think how empty and cold
the sky is, how distant the family,
but of winged seeds blown from a milkweed field
in the opalescent smokes of early

winter ascending toward heaven's blue,
each self orchestrated in one aria
of river and light. And those behind the blue
are watching even now us on the long way.

. . . .

REYNOLDS PRICE

The Dream of a House

There seems no question the house is mine.
I'm told it first at the start of the tour—
"This is yours, understand. Meant for you.
Permanent." I nod gratitude,
Containing the flower of joy in my mouth—
I knew it would come if I waited, in time.
It's now all round me—and I catalog blessings
Tangible as babies: the floors wide teak
Boards perfectly joined, the walls dove plaster.
At either end a single picture,
Neither a copy—Piero's *Nativity*
With angel glee-club, Vermeer's pregnant girl
In blue with her letter. Ranks of books
On the sides—old Miltons, Tolstoys, *Wuthering*
Heights, Ackermann's *Oxford*. A holograph
Copy of Keats's "To Autumn." All roles
Of Flagstad, Leontyne Price in order
On tape, with photographs. Marian Anderson
At Lincoln Memorial, Easter 1939.
A sense of much more, patiently humming.
My guide gives me that long moment,
Then says "You've got your life to learn
This. I'll show you the rest."

I follow and the rest is normal house.
Necessary living quarters—clean,
With a ship's scraped-bone economy. Bedroom
Cool as a cave, green bath,
Steel kitchen. We end in a long
Bright hall, quarry-tiled—
Long window at the far end
On thick woods in sunlight.
The guide gives a wave of consignment—
"Yours"—though he still hasn't smiled.
I ask the only question I know—

"Alone?" He waits, puzzled maybe
(For the first time I study him—a lean man,
Ten years my junior, neat tan clothes:
A uniform?). So I say again
"Alone?—will I be here alone?"
Then he smiles with a breadth that justifies his wait.
"Not from here on," he says. "That's ended too."
But he doesn't move to guide me farther.
I stand, thinking someone will burst in on us
Like a blond from a cake; and I reel through
Twenty-six years of candidates,
Backsliders till now. Silence stretches
Till he points to a closed door three steps
Beyond us.

I cannot go. After so much time—
Begging and vigils. He takes my elbow
And pulls me with him to an ordinary door,
Black iron knob. I only stand.
He opens for me—an ordinary hall
Closet: shelf lined with new hats,
Coats racked in corners. In the midst
Of tweeds and seersuckers, a man is
Nailed to a T-shaped rig—
Full-grown, his face eyelevel with mine,
Eyes clamped. He has borne on a body
No stronger than mine every
Offense a sane man would dread—
Flailed, pierced, gouged, crushed—
But he has the still bearable sweet
Salt smell of blood from my own finger,
Not yet brown, though his long
Hair is stiff with clots, flesh blue.

The guide has never released my arm.
Now he takes it to the face. I don't resist.
The right eyelid is cool and moist.
I draw back slowly and turn to the guide.

Smile more dazzling than the day outside,
He says "Yours. Always."

I nod my thanks, accept the key.
From my lips, enormous, a blossom spreads
At last—white, smell strong as
New iron chain: gorgeous,
Lasting, fills the house.

.   .   .   .

From "Nine Mysteries"

Annunciation

The Angel Gabriel was sent from God to a city in Galilee
named Nazareth to a virgin promised to a man named Joseph
of the house of David. The virgin's name was Mary. Coming in
on her he said "Rejoice, beloved! The Lord is with you."
LUKE 1: 26–28

The angel tries to imagine *need.*
Till now he has not stood near a girl—
Odd generals, magistrates, prophets in skins—
And since his mission is to cry "Beloved!"
And warn of the coming down on her
Of absolute need, he pauses to study
Her opaque hands—both open toward him—
And strains to know what need could draw
The Heart of Light to settle on this
Dun child, clay-brown, when curved space
Burns with willing vessels compounded of air.
He feels he is failing; is balked by skin,
Hair, eyes dense as coal.
"Beloved" clogs his throat. He blinks.
Nothing needs this. He has misunderstood.

The girl though has passed through shock to honor
And begins to smile. She plans to speak.
Her dry lips part. "*Me.*" She nods.

The low room fills that instant with dark
Which is also wind—a room not two
Of her short steps wide, plugged with dark
(Outside it is three, March afternoon).
In the cube, black as a cold star's core,
One small point shines—her lean face
Licked by a joy no seraph has shown,
An ardor of need held back for this
And bound to kill.
                        But slowly she dims,
The room recovers, she opens a fist.

The angel can speak. "Rejoice, beloved!"

The girl laughs one high note, polite—
Cold news—then kneels by her cot to thank him.

Resurrection

*Mary the Magdalene turned and saw Jesus standing, not that she
knew it was Jesus.*

> *Jesus said to her "Woman, why cry? Whom do you want?"*
>
> *She thinking it was the gardener said to him "Sir, if you
carried him off tell me where you put him and I'll take him."*
>
> *Jesus said to her "Mary."*
>
> *Turning she said to him in Hebrew "Rabboni" which means
Teacher.*
>
> *Jesus said to her "Don't touch me for I haven't yet gone up to
the Father. But go to my brothers and tell them 'I'm going up to
my Father and your Father, my God and your God.'"*

JOHN 20: 14–17

She's come a last time before day to touch him.
Last and first. Till now she has not—
Though till him what she'd known
Was ways to touch, valuable ways
That got her her life: small life

Promising to end, early rest.
Friday they'd only had time to loop him
In myrrh and aloes with linen strips
When Sabbath stopped them.
                              She's filled thirty hours
With hope of this, a private end—
Five minutes alone at the instant of day
To find his face and feet, wash them.
Then the gang of others, parceling him
(She'd hid all Saturday to plan in secret,
To come here unfollowed in Sunday dark).
She even knows her way round guards,
Her way to move rock—her old way, her—
And have her chance and be gone by light
To whatever house will feed her now.

No guard, no rock. Her fast hands
Scratch at the small thick dark. No body
On the ledge—blank yards of linen, stiff
With blood.
            Late, she thinks. She says "*Again.*"
All her life she has missed her needs
By moments. Simple needs.
                           She shudders as demons
Pluck at her face—blind cocks, horn beaks
That will gouge till they find old holes
In. They touch her at least, know her slick skin.
She half-grins in welcome, slumps on the ledge.
Hot padding. She gnaws it.
                          What she does not know—
Outside it is day. In the garden he hunts
Her, her first. He is stunned—
Calf, wet colt, boy dredged from sleep.
Each step toward her, he burns with fresh blood
Rushing his legs. He feels he has won
All he swore to win, can face her now.

When she steps from the grave, sees him, knows,
He will not let her touch him.

. . . .

The Annual Heron

December 27th, down for breakfast,
Profoundly fondued from the previous night,
I raise the blinds on panes broadcasting
Cold, a signal—clear sky, sun,
Pond still liquid though thickening
At the rim, and the annual heron
Fifty yards beyond me in rigid profile,
Four feet high, slate gray,
One flat eye, cocked in every cell
(Neck out, legs locked), hunting again:
Fish or me?

His tenth year with me—the fish or me.
I know because when I saw him first,
I wrote him down in my first novel
Which was ending then. He still stands
There, page 169, proffered oasis
For a couple too gorged on mutual
Misery to take his option—consolation *in situ*
Or an emblem of flight, contented self-service.
Hungrier then myself, I wondered;
And now, nine visits later,
Hollow as a whistle, I press this annual
Appearance for a meaning beyond the obvious—
Migration.

After three, four years of two-day visits,
The message seemed identical with Yeats's wild swans'—
Mortality, mine; that chances were fair
A bird as fragile as a cuckoo clock might

(Despite yearly odysseys through air thick
With threat, toward waters jelled with poison)
Outlast iron me, revisit this pond
In my total absence. Or even the reverse—
Yeats again, *Lapis Lazuli*:
"Over them flies a long-legged bird,
A symbol of longevity."
—Bird's or mine though?

A year ago it seemed suddenly mine.
He arrived late—mid-January—
One day ahead of a hard cold wave
(Clanging air, foot of snow, pond dense as ingots)
And stood on the surface, staring at fish
Safe as houses from what I assumed was
Desperate need. Or took slow
Aimless steps, maladroit as
A nineteenth-century German child's
Toy, all gears and contingency—
First *this*, then *that*. And wouldn't leave—
Waited four, five days as the weather screwed down:
Zero for the first time in my life here.
Mornings I'd come down to see him there,
Condensed a notch farther by night, famine
But hunting still—fish roared in joy,
Their own only enemies. By then his plight
Seemed roughly mine—vital provisions
In clean showcases, permanently sealed—
So I tried to let him at them: coated, booted
Myself and fumbled with a log to stave
A usable hole in the ice. Sealed
Also. All I managed was scaring him
Out of sight (slow agonized ascent,
Unlikely, ludicrous as the doomed Ornithopter).
Two brief consolations—that mere exercise might
Warm him a little; that maybe
He was gone on finally, roused by my impotence
From some odd equinoctial daze—

Fish under glass!—and packed off to Georgia
Or the Everglades.

No. Next morning (sixth day of the freeze)
He was not on view, but when I got home
At five o'clock—light nearly dead—he was
There on thicker ice, stiffer, shrunk,
Bitter as a cast-iron flamingo,
Facing me. Seeing what?
Transmitting what signal? *Hunger to death.*

Plea or command?
Plea I decided and took from my freezer
A twenty-inch trout (gift from a friend's
Weekend in the Smokies), stiff as cordwood,
And thawed it in the oven—instant stench
Which the furniture blotted for slow release.
Then I suited up again and moved down toward him
Gingerly (my normal mode though
I'm awful at it, scare a number of targets—
Was he here to teach that? a hunter's
Tread?). He seemed to watch me head-on
From the center where he stood suspended over
Twelve feet of water; but if he saw,
He'd abandoned fear as a luxury—
Better to risk this absurd approach
Than exert one calorie of life on flight.
I stopped at the edge though the water would have borne
Me as easily as him, stooped and slid
The trout toward him, bowled it perfectly
A foot from his feet, then gingerly left—
Not looking back on my charity, his gratitude
Till indoors again behind my own glass.
He was there, unmoved, facing the trout but
Blind or stupefied or too weak
To eat or had to have water
To lubricate a swallow or didn't like trout.
I watched long enough to register nightfall—

I could stand another ten minutes,
Watch him folded in darkness
Or fix my own supper (less desirable than trout)
Or take quilts out to bundle him up,
Force-feed him before his own supper
Froze again.

I ate, watched the news; and by early
Morning he was still out of sight,
No sign of the trout though—hopeful omen—
Yet after coffee I went down to check.
From my end of the snowy ice to where he'd
Last stood were crowded dog tracks
And, on his site, a small handful
Of lilac-gray feathers. No beak, no bone
Of bird or trout. I'd only succeeded
In luring the neighborhood clutch of hyenas,
Standard lethal suburban equipment.
I knelt for a feather—strong wing
Vane—and thought that if that was the meaning,
The message straining through years for delivery,
Then it came as no news, cliché oily
As an oleograph moonrise. Why should nature labor
Through staggering waste to state in mammoth
Semaphore the conclusion any
Baby draws once it's cleared the sphincter
Vaginalis?—*We tear what we touch.*
I dropped the feather and climbed home,
Satisfied.

A normal year passed—normal quota of reminders
That the sentence held (some devious
And eloquent, all wasteful as
The heron episode).

He rises from death. Here anyhow
He stands, eleven months later
In the shallows at my end, facing

Me plainly. What am I meant
To do with my first exposure
To resurrection, at year's dead end,
Before my breakfast? (I manage to recall
That resurrections, like natural births,
Have a habit of dawning in the pre-breakfast
Deserts, roses aghast.) First,
I tell myself it's an accident—
A similar bird on the same flight-path.
That holds me long enough to boil a kettle,
But then I remember a way of establishing
Whether I'm confronted by chance or worse—
By a serious note sounded on air
Clear enough to bear it straight at my eyes,
When I've twiddled these chinking metaphors
(Mortality, Immortality) ten years.
My old heron had something wrong with
His knee (is it called a knee? elbow?
Wrist?)—a knot or tumor
Size of a walnut, stained darker
Than the leg. I decide not to check
Precipitously. In fact, I don't
Look out again. I have my breakfast,
Then carefully search *Britannica*
For firm ground to stand on—
Life span of the great blue heron,
Migration. There's ample word on plumage,
Distribution, abundance ("Herons are the most
Cosmopolitan family"), relations with man
("Members of this order are considered to be
Either beneficial or neutral in respect
To the human economy"), feeding habits,
Vocalization ("Many of the ciconiiforms
Are rather silent," which comes as relief—
The chance mine may speak has seemed
At least even); but no help
At all on maximum age, senility
Or the wintering routes of Atlantic

Seaboard members of the family. What is
Unexpected is the constant reference to
Family—"An outstanding feature
In ciconiiform behaviour is gregariousness.
Even when the mode of obtaining food
Necessitates solitude . . . the tendency is
For reassembly at the end of day"
Though mine, or the long succession of mine,
Stays through nights however arctic:
Loyal, alone, next to me.

Hatted and scarfed, I finally look—
He hasn't moved a visible atom
In forty-five minutes. And doesn't move as
The door slams shut and I start
Toward him. But he's watching me,
Not water or the road—unless he's blind
Or some flawless decoy or angel
Or demon or symptom of lunacy; mine,
At last. I walk to within twenty yards
Of the pond—normal racket of dry leaves,
Sticks. At the noise, I know I'm volunteering,
Offering myself for whatever's next
(Which later will sound like symptom number-two
But then—in bristling winter light
By four still acres of cold
Brown water ringed with chalk-
White bones of sycamores,
Sepulchral cedars—was the rational course).
I walk on. He has the knot on his right
Knee. It's grown—size of an oak
Gall now; is it killing him?
With a speed, calm as perfect, his head
Leaves me, flings out from its coil,
Pierces water silently and rises with
A five-inch brim, lets it quiver
In my sight an instant, eats it.
So I step forward another five yards;

And he bears the nearness for maybe four seconds,
Profile to me. Credible angel—
He gives a first wide fan of wings;
Then rises, trailing legs like crutches.
Till he's half-gone, I hear his oaring
Like lashes—*hrr, hrr*: no pain
Ensues.

So left with that—actual phoenix
At the edge of my yard, possessed of new
Grace since his nocturnal skirmish with
The local dingoes; entirely acceptable
Minister of silence—I climb to the otherwise
Empty house and make for myself
An oracle from his mute persistence
Through volumes of air, corrosive years—
Endurance is fed: here, in time.
Therefore endure. Then make another—
You hope in vain. The heart is fed
Only where I go when I leave you here.
Follow me.

. . . .

From "Days and Nights: A Journal"

24.   Rest

Day calm and gray as a pewter plate,
Chartreuse new leaves in billows at the glass;
Broody wrens commanding the eaves
With a purpose pure as the laws of ice;

And me—laid-up from the frantic last days
Of a term of students famished as sand,
Winning as fawns (their smoky ordnance
At Milton and God still litters my floor).

Rest. The promise of a week like silt
In a sweetwater delta, stirred only by minnows
And the mutter of each slow skin of nacre
As it welds to the pearl of a somnolent oyster—

Mindless companion while I too mutter
Round my gritty core, this ruined glad life.

31.   The Dream of Refusal

I've come on foot through dark dense as fur
(Clean, dry but pressed to my mouth)
To find my mother's father's house
In Macon, N.C. I know he's been dead
Since she was a girl, but—stronger—I know
A secret's here I must face to live.

At the end of seventy miles I see it,
Though the dark's unbroken and no light shows
From any tall window or the open door.
I pull myself through the rooms by hand—
All dead, empty, no stick or thread,
Not the house I loved in childhood

And no more hint of a vital secret
Than noon sun stamps on a working hand.
I forget my life is staked on this hunt,
That these walls store dried acts or words
To kill or save precisely me who pass
Fool-fearless and out again—the yard, lighter dark.

I'm leaving the place and have reached the thicket
Of shrubs near the road. I step through the last
Clear space that can still be called my goal—
My mother's father's home in Macon.
I lift my foot to enter freedom
(And death? I no longer think of death).

Behind me I feel a quick condensation—
Sizable presence barely humming
In furious motion. Fear thrusts up me
Like rammed pack-ice. But I know again
Why I'm here at all, and slowly I turn
Onto whatever deadly shadow waits.

What seems a small man—blackhaired, young—
Crouches in yellow glow he makes,
A smoke from his skin. I know at once
His motion is dance; that he dances every
Instant he breathes, huddled ecstatic.
His hands are empty. He beckons me.

I know he will make his thrust any moment;
I cannot guess what aim it will take.
Then as—appalled—I watch him quiver,
He says "Now you must learn the bat dance."
I know he has struck. It is why I came.
In one long silent step, I refuse and turn toward home.

I will walk all night. I will not die of cancer.
Nothing will make me dance in that dark.

. . . .

I Am Transmuting

I am transmuting. Since you touch my heart,
It gilds inside me. Look, I turn to gold.
Stone I carve, plaster that I paint
Assumes new worth—warnings, praises, glories.
So since your face scored target on my eyes
And I still live, pocked by your barrage,
I move in armor, forged by incantation;
Halt for nothing, nothing harms me now.
I walk on water, walk unscorched through flame;

I kindle light in beggars blind from birth,
And my warm spit sucks poison from hot sores.

after Michelangelo Buonarotti

. . . .

From "Days and Nights 2: A Journal"

23.   15 March 1987 (To W.S.P.)

Today I've lived my father's life—
Fifty-four years, forty-two days.

Father—there beyond that wall—
I beg to pass you, beg your plea

For excess life: more earthly luck
Or a longer sentence in the old appalling

Gorgeous jail in which you craved
My vivid mother, made my bones.

24.   16 March 1987 (To W.S.P.)

Given. Today I exceed your life
By an extra day of gray warm rain;

And there just now through glass on the air,
My heron soars in to work the pond—

"Symbol of longevity" here this year
Long past his usual winter stay

Despite two snows and his mythic age:
Tall slate-blue spirit, never leave.

From "Six Memoranda"

6. Farewell with Photographs

Time is mainly pictures,
After a while is only pictures.

Five years, for instance—all but two thousand days—
Will resolve to a few dozen pictures in time:
Of which, if ten give long-range pleasure to their veterans,
Thanks are due.

Thanks then for time—
Deep-cut pictures,
Mainly delight.

. . . .

JAMES SEAY

It All Comes Together Outside the Restroom in Hogansville

It was the hole for looking in
only I looked out
in daylight that broadened
as I brought my eye closer.
First there was a '55 Chevy
shaved and decked like old times
but waiting on high-jacker shocks.
Then a sign that said J. D. Hines Garage.
In J. D.'s door was an empty Plymouth
with the windows down and the radio on.
A black woman was singing in Detroit
in a voice that brushed against the face
like the scarf
turning up in the wrong suitcase
long ago after everything came to grief.
What was inside we can only imagine—
men I guess trying to figure what would make it
work again. Beyond them
beyond the cracked engine blocks and thrown pistons
beyond that failed restroom
etched with our acids beyond that American Oil Station
beyond the oil on the ground
the mobile homes all over Hogansville
beyond our longing
all Georgia was green.
I'd had two for the road
a cheap enough thrill
and I wanted to think
I could take only what aroused me.
The interstate to Atlanta was wide open.
I wanted a different life.
So did J. D. Hines. So did the voice on the radio.
So did the man or woman
who made the hole in the window.

The way it works is this:
we devote ourselves to an image
we can't live with and try to kill
anything that suggests it could be otherwise.

. . . .

Think Back

The hummingbird that tried to fly through the glass
of your big window last summer like a plane of light,
was it bringing you a promise?

How long can you hold out in that living room?

When you found the hummingbird, weren't ants working
the channels of its body like spiritual electricians
wiring the wing of a cathedral for miracles?

. . . .

Drilling for Fire

for my students
who have lost sleep over it

Even if it were for real
it would not be a fire worth remembering
or losing sleep over,
not in this stone block—

a mattress maybe, or plaid curtains
someone's mother sent,
but nothing to light up the sky
like a celebration,
nothing that would touch you
and leave a mark

like the girl who has come into your room
while you wait twelve floors down
for the all-clear sign.

At this precise moment
she is pulling the red sweep-second hand
off your clock,
knowing you never needed that fine a reading.

But you do not yet know of your losses;
echoes are entering your head
like sleet drilling an open pond
and someone is saying there is no fire,
no need for water,
return to your room.

You are moving back up the stairwell
to where your door offers back your name.
Inside you realize that things are missing.

Cuff links are gone,
your sleeves flap in the wind from the hall.
Your baby book, your high-school yearbook,
all your scrapbooks are open on the desk
where she has cut your pictures out
and pasted in an invitation to a party
for the misunderstood,
an obsolete flight schedule,
the label from a jar of facial cream,
an ad for a tour of the homes
of movie stars.

You try to remember your face in the pictures.
All that comes to you is the time
you used the thin sweep-second
to see how long you could hold your breath.
Not long enough to suit you.

And all the other that is missing?
On your tape recorder
she has left you clues
to where you can eventually find
the whole cache
if you want it back.
A scavenger hunt that will take
the rest of your life.

Finally she says
she thinks she ought to tell you
she is your mother,
no your sister,
no no the first girl you entered,
no she means your future wife
or your present one or one you lusted after secretly,
or rather a woman
you never knew
and she is waiting for you
in a place you might not recognize
if you decide to come, begging her
to say what else should be forgotten.

You must decide, though,
and tell yourself what kind of recovery you want:

you can go with clues
toward cuff links and buttons,
things you used to hold yourself together,
a measured breath, old preventive devices,
lapsed membership cards,
and other mementoes,

or else you can start on your own
toward her voice.

For the time being
you are in ashes everywhere you turn.
What can you say?

But wait,
the pool of blue in your bed, she says,
will furnish you with words you've denied yourself:
dip your pen there in sleep
and write your life on the wall
in the language of dreams.
The empty ink bottle on the floor—
fill it with small stones and cinders
from along the interstate
as you go on wherever you've told yourself.
Study the reductions that have taken place.
There in the bottle—study your life
as though it were on fire.

. . . .

The Hand That Becomes You

The glove that washed up on the beach,
shake the hand out and wear it home.
It quite becomes you.
The knots you could never master—
clove hitches, carrick bends, Matthew Walkers, Blackwall hitches—
are now yours and instinctively
you start securing things
that might be swept over.
By nightfall you are put in mind of the breasts of port whores
rousing in your palm,
there are flashes of bayside bars, a mixture of foreign tongues.
You find yourself buying heavy wool turtlenecks in dark colors,
calling your dog *mate.*

One morning you wake hungover,
an anchor tattooed on your forearm.
The interior decorator comes and you tell him
do it all nautical. Rigging is installed.
Men begin bringing a great store of food to your cellar
and one morning you feel your hand wince at the sight of cable
coiling around the windlass.
Realizing you are weighing anchor, you tell your hand
eight bells and all is well, all is well!
You pledge your trust in it,
promising never to let it get caught short-handed again.
It comes out of your pocket gladly to cast the mooring away
and you heave forth a mighty blessing of profanities
that astound you and bring joy to the hearts of your shipmates.
They are saying there is a New World out there,
you lucky bastard you, a New World,
islands of spice and fruit and friendly natives
ever willing to give a helping hand.

. . . .

When Once Friends

I can tell this fairly quick,
the two narrative lines sharing a common angle
and there being mist in both instances.
As for why my friend and I
were running a rented fishing boat
through morning fog on dead reckoning,
it was a matter of wanting to arrive early and alone
at the shrimp farm where sea trout
were working along the fence for strays.
More than anything I remember the angle,
something sure and strict in my reading,
of the cabin cruiser that came out of the fog
and crossed our bow close enough for us
to know again it was not our special selves
or anything our wives knew about greyhounds

that had paid us eleven-to-one on two-dollar bets
at the dog track the night before.
A name on the racing form more lyric than the next,
a combination of favored colors in the silks,
the worn luck of the draw,
was what bought us beer in green bottles
instead of cans for the weekend.
The cruiser never looked back
at my friend and me and our luck
rolling in their wake.
The other angle was of a plane in the clouds,
the only time I've ever been ferried by private charter.
Going up through cloud cover
the young pilot said he didn't have radar
and had never been to where I was going,
so we'd have to come back down through the clouds
in a calculated while and look around for a landmark.
His co-pilot pointed to a symbol
for a checkered water tower on the chart.
All I could add to the basic rhopalic of clock,
compass, and radio was another eye,
the one pointing my finger toward the Cessna
that had just slipped through the gauze
of our future like a cruiser
and laid down for the second time in my life
the providential angle.
Those twin incidents were long
ago and whatever has made
my friend remote and finally silent
as he goes about his days
is as hidden to me as the way two such moments
could conform so in texture and geometric circumstance.
One other thing:
after we found the water tower
and were parked on the runway,
the pilot walked around the nose of the plane
to where I was standing with my bags.
He reached up and broke a sleeve of ice

from the leading edge of the wing
and offered half to me.
His co-pilot had forgotten to fill the water jug.
After a few minutes of small talk
he taxied up the runway
lifting into the overcast winter.
I stood there beside the one road leading in,
waiting for my ride and thinking of how the morning
cleared on the wide sound
and we caught the speckled trout
our wives broiled with pimiento and Parmesan,
lemon and parsley.
We drank the beer in green bottles,
saying the wonderful names of the winning hounds
all through the evening.
That was what I remembered that winter day
and what I remember now is both that and the angle—
and standing there on the small runway,
eating the ice of unknowing alone,
its cloud, where we had been.

·   ·   ·   ·   ·   ·   ·

Faith as an Arm of Culture,
Culture as an Arm of Narration

All those miles, the dark water beneath us
as we slept in the wide rows.
From Heathrow, jet-lagging and hugging the left
eight hours into the moors
to walk through the open gate
beside the flower garden and find it—
right where she said on the transatlantic telephone,
my friend Bonnie from Georgia,
away for the weekend with her fiancé in France:
the back door key
up under the mop bucket,
her grandmother's language and habit.

Clouds over Islands

First there was a dream not wholly mine.

I told my friends the dream
comes with the bed, its source a cloud
accumulated in the air surrounding sleep.

Just off the plane, I had dozed on their bed
as they swam in the screened pool, promising
I would like the crabs at Joe's Stone Crabs,
the daughter would be off the phone in my room
shortly, she was in love. The migrant dream
settled around me as the rhythm of the laps they swam
defined the rhythm of my breathing.

When I woke it took their voices
from beside the pool for me to know
I had breathed the dream
from the cloud above their private island of sleep.

The dream itself does not matter
in its particulars,
not even to my friends.
Nor could I have told it clearly, its cloud
so tropic and brief in my life.

I told them of a family I knew in Ohio
who bought the childhood furniture
of a famous astronaut, his little bed and mattress,
the strange vast air
in which the family's daughter began to dream.

Then together we remembered confusions
in the expired air over beds we had held
in hotels, hospitals, the compartments of trains,
or rooms of senility where our grandfathers called back

the gifts they had given us,
how sometimes still we rise from sleep in beds
where no friends have breathed dreams
we can enter without fear,
how we stumble to our belongings,
trying to make sure of what we left there.

. . . .

Where Our Voices Broke Off

From the porch, if they hold to what there is
no need to imagine, they can color the hedge,
the sound, the lighthouse with its pattern of black
and white lozenges, or the air over the island
and anything lofted in its translations.
My sons turn their brushes instead to the chronic
bad dreams of the race, fixing them at random
in the watercolors of flame or collision.
They are old hands at apostrophe.
The shrimper's son from across the road tries a few circles
and then begins the outline of a boat.

Last night from this porch I looked up
with my wife and friends to our share
of the galaxy, whorled pure and free of mainland lights.
I felt our voices drawn out into the dark
and it seemed to me the round island was a stone
turning beneath us, grinding our voices with the shells
of shrimp in the kitchen pail, the quilts by the door,
the hyphens in the names of boats at anchor—all of it drawn
and turning under the stone—the drums of paint
for the lighthouse diamonds, the bright water that breaks
on shoals and jetties, whatever yields to silence, ground
with our voices and spread like grist across the spaces.

One of the Dippers brought us out of silence
and we began working our way through the known.

For the constellations we could not name
we imagined *Cricket's Knee, Bill & Doris' Blown Electric Range,*
Anne's New Rod & Reel, Tommy's Measles, and so on
until we all were found.
We called it The Myth of the New Understanding.
It was a way of turning from the silence beyond the porch
railing, the silence in the hedge along the road
and out across the sound to the lighthouse.
It was a way of understanding the lights
burning their codes through darkness.

The boat is colored yellow and the water blue.
It is headed to the left of the paper,
under what appears clear weather.
Toward dawn we saw his father make fast the mooring
and load his catch into a skiff.
I do not know if he looks up at the stars at sea
and wonders what is at the farthest reach of darkness
or if he dwells on whether the shrimp are vanishing.
I do not know if he has told his son of the silent migrations.
He declined the beer.
We bought the shrimp still moiling in the bucket.

•   •   •   •   •   •   •

Audubon Drive, Memphis

There's a black and white photo of Elvis
and his father Vernon in their first swimming pool.
Elvis is about twenty-one and "Heartbreak Hotel"
has just sold a million.
When he bought the house,
mainly for his mother Gladys they say,
it didn't have a pool,
so this is new.
The water is up to the legs of Vernon's trunks
and rising slowly as he stands there
at attention almost.

Elvis is sitting or kneeling on the bottom,
water nearly to his shoulders,
his face as blank and white
as the five feet of empty poolside at his back.
The two of them are looking at the other side
of the pool and waiting for it to fill.
In the book somewhere
it says the water pump is broken.
The garden hose a cousin found is not in the frame,
but that's where the water is coming from.
In the background over Vernon's head you can see
about three stalks of corn
against white pickets in a small garden
I guess Gladys planted.
You could press a point and say that in the corn
and the fence, the invisible country
cousin and mother, the looks on Elvis's and Vernon's
faces, the partly filled pool, we can read
their lives together, the land
they came from, the homage they first thought
they owed the wealth beginning to accumulate,
the corny songs and films,
and that would be close but not quite central.
Closer than that is the lack
of anything waiting in the pool we'd be
prompted to call legend
if we didn't know otherwise.
They're simply son and father wondering if it's true
they don't have to drive a truck
tomorrow for a living.
But that's not it either.
What it reduces to is the fact that most of us
know more or less everything
that is happening to them
as though it were a critical text
embracing even us and our half-mawkish
geographies of two or three word obituaries:
in the case of Kennedy, for example, I was walking

across a quad in Oxford,
Mississippi; King's death too caught me in motion,
drifting through dogwood in the Shenandoah.
As for Elvis,
there were some of us parked outside a gas station
just over the bridge from Pawley's Island
with the radio on.
That's enough.
I know the differences.
But don't think they're outright.
The photo is 1034 Audubon Drive, Memphis,
and then it's Hollywood,
still waiting for the pool to fill.

· · · · · · · ·

Mountains by Moonlight

The postcard artist Harry Martin
could have gone to Mars
and not found a better full moon
for his Mountains by Moonlight.
It looks like a photograph
that's been hand-tinted and stars added.
When they were young
our grandparents sent it home
wishing everyone was there in the space
for writing messages.
The matte finish softens the moonlight
to where it's almost melancholy.
We don't know whether to lie down
and embrace our aloneness together on earth
or fly to the moon.
It's pure nature,
not a Model T or AAA sign in sight,
but we know that outside the frame
the technology's in place for flight,
organ transplants, just about anything

you could imagine.
We know that beyond the mountains by moonlight
there is an architecture
our grandparents had to leave finally
in the same way they left these mountains.
We know that when we draw arrows,
as they did, to hotel windows
it's both to separate ourselves
from the sheer sameness of things *my room*
was here and yet double the evidence
we were part of that sameness
my room was there.
Once for a magazine article
I located Scott Fitzgerald's room
at the Grove Park Inn in Asheville
by standing in the parking lot
and counting up to the window
he had x'd on a postcard.
From the terrace he could see
the lights of Highland Hospital
where Zelda thought she was talking
to Christ and William the Conqueror and Mary Stuart.
Not even the mountains by moonlight
could put him to sleep,
so he took Luminal and Amytal
and a young married woman from Memphis.
Two years later he was in Hollywood.
We don't know if it was silliness
or loneliness that prompted the postcard
he sent to himself at the Garden of Allah
where he had rooms.
When they came home they brought us honey
in small jars shaped like bears,
assembly-line tom-toms with rubber heads,
cities we could shake into blizzards.
They asked if we got the cards.
Next year it would be palm trees
and a crescent moon.

We couldn't imagine them under those moons
with anything other than hearts
lifting to the broadened horizon.
We couldn't imagine them as having ever doubted
the light as they found it.

. . . .

JONATHAN WILLIAMS

An Aubade from Verlaine's Day

for Alfred Stieglitz

the cloud in my head
wide to the edge of the world

the level cloud
that fills the Valley of the Little Tennessee
from Ridgepole to Rabun Bald

the laughter of
the Lord God Bird
Who pecks
berries
from the
dogwood

makes these two clouds
one, one eye
open

· · · · · · · ·

Still Water

for Lorine Niedecker (1903–1970)

she seined words
as other stars
or carp

laconic as
a pebble
in the Rock River

along the bank
where the peony flowers
fall

her tall friend
the pine tree
is still there

to see

. . . .

My Quaker-Atheist Friend,
Who Has Come to This Meeting-House since 1913,
Smokes
& Looks Out over the Rawthey to Holme Fell

what do you do
anything for?

you do it
for what the mediaevals would call
something like
the *Glory of God*

doing it for money
that doesn't do it;

doing it for vanity,
that doesn't do it;

doing it to justify a disorderly life,
that doesn't do it

Look at Briggflatts here . . .

It represents the best
that the people were able to do

they didn't do it for gain;
in fact, they must have
taken a loss

whether it is a stone next to a stone
or a word next to a word,
it is the *glory*—
the simple craft of it

and money and sex aren't worth
bugger-all, not
bugger-all

solid, common, *vulgar* words

the ones you can touch,
the ones that yield

and a respect for the music . . .

what else can you tell 'em?

. . . .

Symphony No. 5, in C Sharp Minor

"How blessed, how blessed a tailor to be!
Oh that I had been born a commercial traveller and engaged as
baritone at the Opera! Oh that I might give my Symphony its
first performance fifty years after my death!"
—Mahler, 1904

I. FUNERAL MARCH

Mahler, from his studio on the 11th floor of the
Hotel Majestic, New York City, hears the cortège of a
fireman moving up Central Park West:

one roll of the drum

one road where the wind storms, where
Cherubim sing birds' songs
with human faces and hold the world
in human hands and
drift on the gold road

where black wheels smash
all

one roll of the drum

II. STORMILY AGITATED

to be a block of flowers
in a wood

to be mindlessly in flower
past understanding

to be shone on
endlessly

to be *there*, there
and blessed

III. SCHERZO

one two three
one two three

little birds waltz to and fro
in the piano

at Maiernigg on the
Wörthersee

and up the tree:
cacophony

one two three

IV. ADAGIETTO

one feels
one clematis petal
fell

its circle
is all

glimmer on this pale
river

Schoenberg: "I should
even have liked to observe
how Mahler
knotted his tie,

and should have found that
more interesting and instructive
than learning how
one of our musical bigwigs composes
on a quote sacred subject
unquote

. . . An apostle
who does not glow
preaches heresy."

his tie was knotted
with éclat
on the dead run!

. . . .

Dealer's Choice
and the Dealer Shuffles

for William Burroughs

I saw the Chattahoochee River get a haircut.
I saw Fidel Castro flow softly towards Apalachicola, Florida.

I saw a bank of red clay integrate with Jesuits.
I saw Bob Jones Bible University used to make baked flamingos.

I saw the Governor of Mississippi join the NAACP.
I saw a black gum tree refuse to leaf and go to jail.

I saw the DAR singing "*We Shall Overcome!*"
I saw Werner von Braun knitting gray (and brown) socks for the National
    Guard.

I saw the Motto of Alabama: "IT'S TOO WET TO PLOUGH!"
I saw God tell Adam: "WE DARE DEFEND OUR RIGHTS!"

I saw the City of Albany fried in deep fat.
I saw eight catfish star on Gomorrah TV.

I saw "THE INVASION OF THE BODY-SNATCHERS" at the Tyger Drive-In.
I saw William Blake grow like a virus in the sun.

I saw the South suckin hind titty.
I saw the North suckin hind titty.

I saw a man who saw these too
And said though strange they were all true.

Postface:

"There was a crow sat on a clod—
And now I've finished my sermon, thank God."

.   .   .   .

Blue Ball Blues

for Paul Goodman

O, Mr. Chemist, please let me buy
350 pounds of premium Kentucky KY,

cause it's a dry season
for the reason

Anglo-Saxon sex glands
are awry . . .

Arise, arise and come
to Perineum

("*the more you come*
the more you can")

Let not your Sword sleep in your Hand
and we shall smear Petroleum
on England's Groin
& Pleasant Gland!

.   .   .   .

Who Is Little Enis?

Little Enis is
"one hunnert an' 80lbs of
dynamite
with a 9-inch
fuse"

his real name is
Carlos Toadvine
which his wife Irma Jean
pronounces *Carlus*

Carlos says
Toadaveenie is a eyetalyun name,
used to be lots of 'em
round these parts

Ed McClanahan is the World's Leading Little Enis Freak
and all this information comes to you from a weekend in Winston
with Big Ed telling the lore of Lexington, Kentucky,
which is where Enis has been hanging it out for years and years,
at Boots Bar and Giuseppe's Villa and, now, The Embers,
pickin' and singin' rockabilly style

Carlus ain't what he was
according to Irma Jean's accounts
(and even to his own):

he was sittin' there one night in the kitchen at home
tellin' stories and talkin' trash about Irma Jean—
with her right there with her hair put up in them pink plastic curlers—
about how these days how he likes to pop it to her dog-style
just now and again and how she likes it pretty damn well
when they wander all over the house
and end up in the living room corner—
"I'm just afraid Carlus will run us out the door and down the street
opposite the automatic laundry . . ."

The 9-inch fuse hung down Enis' left leg
is called, familiarly,
Ol' Blue

Ol' Blue used to be in the pink!—
way in . . .

Blue has a head on him like a tom-cat
and ribs like a hongry hound

and he used to get so hard
a cat
couldn't
scratch it . . .

but now that Enis has the cirrhosis
and takes all thesehere harmones
Ol' Blue just don't
stand up
like a little man
and cut the mustard
anymore

but Enis will smile and say
let's all have a drink, maybe I can drown thatthere liver of ours,
it's no bigger'n a dime nohow anymore, it just floats in there . . .

Hey, Blue, let's shake that thang!
Turn a-loose this oldie
by my boy Elvis—
a golden oldie!
let's go, Blue!

And off they go
into the Wild Blue
Yonder in the Blue
Grass . . .

Carlos & Blue,
thinking of you . . .

Hail & Farewell!

.   .   .   .

Orange County Blues

(To the Tune: "Keep Your Chicken Lickin'")

fresh, ford-run-over
possum
plus a six-pak

that's the springtime seven-coarse greasy spoon blue-plate
special in Chapel
Hill according to Bill
Harmon, poet & possum
consumer

this spring weather's
tough on possums

they get out in the middle lane
and just get nicked
and take a long time to succumb

the possum,
like the Literary Life,
it's a little rank
lately . . .

. . . .

From "In the Piedmont"

3.   Red Pig Barbecue #2, Concord

Irene:
Whuddya git fer Christmas, Bernice?

Bernice:
Everything I wanted: a rifle and a blender!

6.   The Anthropophagites Get Down
     on a Barbecue Sign on
     Highway NC 107 South of Hamlet

EAT

300 FEET

. . . .

A Rhyme without End for Howard Finster
about How It All Began in the Country near Lookout

I thought at first of swarms of bees . . .
But, sure enough, it was God Who was shooting the breeze,
looking about in thishere grove of red trees,

Who said to Howard (down there on his knees),
"Howard, your warm arm, please,
what we need down here is a man who 'sees'
the glory stored in *breeze* and *trees*
and what art there is in words to bring folks ease."

Swarm for the Lord like bees!
Sing like honey on its knees!

. . . .

Daddy Bostain, the Moses of the Wing Community Moonshiners, Laments from His Deathbed the Spiritual Estate of One of His Soul-Saving Neighbors

God bless her pore
little ol
dried up
soul!

jest make
good kindlin wood
fer Hell . . .

. . . .

Aunt Dory Ellis, of Penland, Remembers When She Fell in Her Garden at the Home Place and Broke Her Hip in 19 and 56

the sky was high,
white clouds passing
by, I lay
a hour in that petunia patch

hollered,
and knew I was out of whack

Miss Lucy Morgan Shows Me a Photograph
of Mrs. Mary Grindstaff Spinning Wool on the High Wheel

Miss Lucy tells that one day
a visitor asked Mrs. Grindstaff
"What are you doing?"

she said "Spinning."

the tourist said
"Why doesn't it break?"

she said "Because I don't let it."

the charred heart does not break in Appalachia, they
have not let it . . .

the loom hums

there

· · · · · · · ·

The Ancient of Days

would that I
had known Aunt Cumi
Woody

C-u-m-i, pronounced
Q-my

she lived in the Deyton Bend Section of Mitchell
County, North Carolina many years ago

there is one of Bayard Wootten's photographs of her
standing there with her store-bought
teeth, holding a coverlet

she sheared her sheep, spun
and dyed her yarn in vegetable dyes,
and wove the coverlet

in indigo, the brown from walnut roots,
red from madder, green from hickory ooze, first,
then into the indigo (the blue pot)

Cumi, from the Bible
(St. Mark 5:41)

Talitha Cumi:
"*Damsel, I say unto thee, arise!*"

she is gone, she
enjoyed her days

. . . .

A Valediction for My Father, Ben Williams (1898–1974)

all the old things
are gone now

and the people are
different

About the Poets

· · · · · · · ·

Each of these brief essays presents commentary on the poet's work, as well as biographical information; whenever possible, some larger aspect of contemporary North Carolina poetry is also addressed. For each poet, a selected bibliography is included; in keeping with this anthology's focus on full-length original books of poems published between 1973 and 1993, only those publications are listed.

BETTY ADCOCK

"You can go back," Betty Adcock declares in the first line of the first poem in this collection, boldly contradicting North Carolina's most famous literary native. You *can* go home again, physically and in poetry; and many of these fifteen poets do just that, returning to their places of origin, reworking the memorable evidence. But—as Wolfe perhaps meant, and Adcock surely shows—the return is not an easy one, no soft-focus nostalgia trip: these are the places they longed to escape when young, "to army, city, anyplace far. / We took any road out we could take." The distances between *then* and *now*, and the intervening years of experience, create an especially powerful tension in Adcock's poems.

In many ways, Betty Adcock is the prototypical contemporary North Carolina poet. She was born in a small town: in her case, in 1938 in San Augustine, Texas, a place so remote that she describes her childhood there as growing up "in the nineteenth century." Eventually, she emigrated to the big city: she married Don Adcock in 1957 and moved with him to Raleigh, where he became assistant director of music at North Carolina State University. She raised a family and worked for a while at nonacademic jobs: for ten years she was a copywriter and creative director for an advertising firm. She has taught poetry writing at various workshops and conferences and schools: currently, she is Kenan Writer in Residence at Meredith College.

But above all, Adcock worked steadily at her poems, publishing them in many magazines and in three volumes, each better than the last. Her poetry is distinctive for its vulnerable but tough voice, its quick wit, its quiet formal accomplishment, and above all its relentless pursuit of what the first poem in her first book called "Identity," the lost self that keeps leading her back to the landscape and relatives and stories of deep East Texas, "knowing there's no place else. Not anywhere."

Walking Out. Baton Rouge: Louisiana State University Press, 1975.
Nettles. Baton Rouge: Louisiana State University Press, 1983.
Beholdings. Baton Rouge: Louisiana State University Press, 1988.

As for every poet in this book, for A. R. Ammons a case could be made that he is not a "North Carolina poet" at all. For three decades, he has lived in Ithaca, New York, where he is Goldwin Smith Professor of Poetry at Cornell University. During that time, his books have been published by New York houses, and his many prizes—among them two National Book Awards, the Bollingen Prize, and a Mac-Arthur Fellowship—have been conferred by the Northern literary-intellectual establishment. And above all, his poems are often philosophical or conceptual in nature and don't seem localized at all, unless that place is his Ithaca backyard or nearby brooks and falls and paths.

And yet, as one of his short poems begins, "I went back / to my old home"—not just literally, for family funerals in eastern North Carolina, but in memory, in language, in the very cadence of his voice and lines. In fact, many of the salient characteristics of Ammons's work—a prevailing solitude, an appetite for the sublime, a fear of death and oblivion, a self-deprecating sense of humor, a microscopic interest in the natural world and its cycles—are at least partly the result of having grown up in poverty on a North Carolina farm during the Depression. Naturally, Ammons's feelings toward his "home country" are mixed; but as he writes in "Easter Morning," "I cannot leave this place, for / for me it is the dearest and the worst, / it is life nearest to life which is / life lost: it is my place."

A. R. Ammons was born in Whiteville, North Carolina, in 1926. He served in the navy and returned to his native state to take a degree in science from old Wake Forest College. In subsequent years he was principal of the elementary school at Hatteras, a student at the University of California in Berkeley, and (for over a decade) an executive with a glassware firm in southern New Jersey. In the late 1950s and early 1960s, his poems began to appear in magazines and books. They earned him an invitation to read at Cornell, which earned him an invitation to teach at Cornell, where he has been ever since.

Diversifications. New York: W. W. Norton, 1975.
The Snow Poems. New York: W. W. Norton, 1977.
A Coast of Trees. New York: W. W. Norton, 1981.
Worldly Hopes. New York: W. W. Norton, 1982.
Lake Effect Country. New York: W. W. Norton, 1983
Sumerian Vistas. New York: W. W. Norton, 1987.
The Really Short Poems of A. R. Ammons. New York: W. W. Norton, 1990.
Garbage. New York: W. W. Norton, 1993.

On January 20, 1993, Maya Angelou delivered her poem "On the Pulse of Morning" at the inauguration of President Bill Clinton. Though the merits of the poem itself have been debated, one thing cannot be denied: it was an extraordinarily *visible* moment for poetry, one seen and heard by hundreds of thousands in Washington and many millions on television, one that provoked a lot of talk about (and maybe even interest in) poetry. And if anyone could make the most of such a moment, it's Maya Angelou: she has tremendous stage presence and is an inspired reader of her poetry. In fact, if her poems on the page sometimes seem a bit flat, that's because they are less texts to be studied than scripts to be performed. Though the poems in the present selection do read well on the page, they should also be read aloud: Angelou's work is relentlessly oral.

Maya Angelou is the most recent arrival among these North Carolina poets. She moved to the state in 1980 to become a Reynolds Professor at Wake Forest University and lives in Winston-Salem. But her life has been a truly international one: she was born Marguerite Johnson in 1928 in St. Louis and raised in Arkansas, but she has gone on to become a citizen of the world, living and traveling in many places, with diverse achievements in theater, film, music, and television. She is perhaps best known for *I Know Why the Caged Bird Sings*, part of an ongoing series of autobiographical books.

In a recent interview, Angelou comments, "There is, I hope, a thesis in my work: we may encounter many defeats, but we must not be defeated. That sounds goody-two-shoes, I know, but I believe that a diamond is the result of extreme pressure and time. Less time is crystal. Less than that is coal. Less than that is fossilized leaves. Less than that it's just plain dirt. In all my work, in the movies I write, the lyrics, the poetry, the essays, I am saying that we may encounter many defeats—maybe it's imperative that we encounter the defeats—but we are much stronger than we appear to be, and maybe much better than we allow ourselves to be."

Oh Pray My Wings Are Gonna Fit Me Well. New York: Random House, 1975.
And Still I Rise. New York: Random House, 1978.
Shaker, Why Don't You Sing?. New York: Random House, 1983.
I Shall Not Be Moved. New York: Random House, 1990.

JAMES APPLEWHITE

All of the poets in this book exhibit what Guy Owen once called "a deep attachment to place": that's one reason they can be gathered in a volume with a geographical focus. But none is more place-oriented than James Applewhite: from the beginning of his first book, he has written about "places not much in anyone's thoughts, / Wadesboro, Mt. Gilead, Calvary Church." His work is steeped in the memory of such forgotten spots and is in fact a sustained elegy for a landscape and way of life that may be passing away but are preserved in his meditative poems.

Applewhite was born in 1935 in Stantonsburg, a town of a thousand people in eastern North Carolina tobacco country. He was raised there and educated at Duke University (A.B., M.A., and Ph.D.), where he has been teaching since 1972. He lives near the Eno River in northern Durham County. All of these places—his family's farm; the university, with its intellectual life, so far removed from his origins; the river by which he jogs and thinks—have profoundly informed his work, which is at once deeply rooted and yet extremely distanced (by years, by miles, by personal and regional history) from its own roots. For Applewhite, even poems about learning to fly a sailplane become an attempt to attain "clarity of vision" and much-needed perspective on the native landscape below. Even a leaf of tobacco becomes a "topographical map," a "pungent terrain," sweet and yet poisonous.

Applewhite's obsession with landscape extends to his scholarly interests as well: he teaches Romantic poetry at Duke and has written a critical study, *Seas and Inland Journeys: Landscape and Consciousness from Wordsworth to Roethke*, which he describes as "an analysis of the Romantic dialectic between consciousness and its landscape opposite"—a dialectic continued in his own poetry.

> *Statues of the Grass.* Athens: University of Georgia Press, 1975.
> *Following Gravity.* Charlottesville: University Press of Virginia, 1980.
> *Foreseeing the Journey.* Baton Rouge: Louisiana State University Press, 1983.
> *Ode to the Chinaberry Tree and Other Poems.* Baton Rouge: Louisiana State University Press, 1986.
> *River Writing: An Eno Journal.* Princeton, N.J.: Princeton University Press, 1988.
> *Lessons in Soaring.* Baton Rouge: Louisiana State University Press, 1989.
> *A History of the River.* Baton Rouge: Louisiana State University Press, 1993.

GERALD BARRAX

As the very existence of this volume suggests, there is a constant impulse to label and subdivide poets. Gerald Barrax, for example, could be classified as a "North Carolina poet." To deepen the canonical focus, he could be called an "American poet," writing in the best tradition of both Whitman's ecstatic ranginess and Dickinson's oblique distillations. To make that focus more close-up, he could be fixed on the basis of his occupation (academic), his gender (male), or his race (black).

But as any poet would probably say, such pigeonholing—though convenient, perhaps, for anthologies and libraries and universities—is completely incidental to the poetry itself. That's especially true for Gerald Barrax. Though his poems naturally reflect his place and job and gender and race, they are not limited by those contemporary realities. His subjects are ancient and rich ones: myths, the natural world, music, and above all love, which gives his poems a deliciously sensuous texture. Like any good poet, he is looking for his place in the world, for the myth "free of cruelty and lies" that he and his family can live by. Rather than adopting the role of outsider—which, as poet and black man, it would be tempting to do—Barrax is emphatically part of our common world, which can seem so capricious and ruthless and yet, at times, beautiful. "What more," he asks, "could anyone expect of me?"

Gerald Barrax was born in Attalla, Alabama, in 1933. At the age of ten, he and his family moved to Pittsburgh, where he later took his college degrees and also worked as a radio mechanic, postal clerk, and mail carrier. He has taught for several decades at North Carolina State University, where he is now professor of English and editor of *Obsidian II: Black Literature in Review*.

An Audience of One. Athens: University of Georgia Press, 1980.

The Deaths of Animals and Lesser Gods. Lexington, Ky.: Callaloo Poetry Series, 1984.

Leaning Against the Sun. Fayetteville: University of Arkansas Press, 1992.

KATHRYN STRIPLING BYER

Kathryn Stripling Byer's poems are the product of extreme patience, a very welcome quality in these rush-to-publish days. Though her second book, *Wildwood Flower*, won a major national prize—it was the 1992 Lamont Poetry Selection of the Academy of American Poets—it was not something she had just dashed off: one of its poems had appeared in Lee Smith's novel *Fair and Tender Ladies* in 1988, others had been gathered as a chapbook called *Alma* in 1983, and all had been in process since Byer moved to the North Carolina mountains decades ago.

Byer was born in 1944 in Camilla, Georgia, and migrated north to attend Wesleyan College in Macon and then the University of North Carolina at Greensboro, where she took her M.F.A. in 1968; but something kept drawing her to the Blue Ridge Mountains, where her grandmother was born. Eventually she got a teaching position at Western Carolina University in Cullowhee, where she is now poet in residence, and began to discover her subject. "I soon found my imagination being stirred by those mountains, their windy sounds, their atmosphere of mystery and solitude," she says. "Wherever I went, I seemed to hear voices, and eventually out of all the voices grew the one with which I could write about these mountains, the voice of a woman named Alma, solitary, abandoned, strong yet susceptible to the shiftings of season and memory."

Wildwood Flower is Alma's story, bittersweet as the old song from which the title comes. Her world—that of a mountain woman near the turn of the century—is a hard one, besieged by weather and labor and emotional abandonment; but it is also a beautiful one—in the mountain's flowering, in the durable handiwork of the poems' lines and Alma's life, and especially in her exemplary resilient spirit. As Kathryn Stripling Byer says, speaking for her readers, "The voice of Alma has shown me how to wait."

The Girl in the Midst of the Harvest. Lubbock: Texas Tech University Press, 1986.
Wildwood Flower. Baton Rouge: Louisiana State University Press, 1992.

FRED CHAPPELL

One reason for the vigorous state of North Carolina poetry is the presence of inspiring teachers of creative writing at the state's universities. Among the poets in this book, Reynolds Price, Fred Chappell, and James Applewhite each took William Blackburn's celebrated class at Duke, and each has gone on to teach new generations of writers: for example, both Robert Morgan and Kathryn Stripling Byer studied with Chappell at the University of North Carolina at Greensboro.

Chappell has lived and taught in Greensboro for three decades; but he was born in the North Carolina mountains (in Canton, in 1936) and was raised there, and he returns there often in his best work. That work is very diverse: it includes four conventional novels, two novels-in-stories (including *I Am One of You Forever*), two collections of short stories, a collection of critical prose, a reader, and over a dozen books of poems. He is one of our few truly genre-ambidextrous writers: his fiction is first-rate, and his poetry (which earned him the Bollingen Prize in 1985) is astonishing.

It's not just that his poems are *good*, though they are, in the way fine poems are, with original imagery, technical variety, intriguing subject matter, formal variety and mastery, and irresistible verbal and narrative momentum. It's that each new book is an *astonishment*: you simply don't know what Chappell will do next. He's unpredictable, poetically incorrect, an avant-garde reactionary. Not content with the conventional contemporary collection of discrete lyrics, Chappell always makes his poems part of some larger design—a four-book verse-novel in *Midquest*, a medieval tale in *Castle Tzingal*, dramatic prologues and epilogues in *First and Last Words*, lieder cycles in part of *Source*, chiseled classical epigrams in *C*. And the really amazing thing is that, despite this ambitiousness of scope and approach, nobody writes more enjoyable poems than Fred Chappell: he never loses his engaging sense of character, sense of humor, or sense of the fellow human reader.

River. Baton Rouge: Louisiana State University Press, 1975.

Bloodfire. Baton Rouge: Louisiana State University Press, 1978.

Wind Mountain. Baton Rouge: Louisiana State University Press, 1979.

Earthsleep. Baton Rouge: Louisiana State University Press, 1980.

Midquest: A Poem. Baton Rouge: Louisiana State University Press, 1981.
[Gathers the previous four volumes.]

Castle Tzingal. Baton Rouge: Louisiana State University Press, 1984.

Source. Baton Rouge: Louisiana State University Press, 1985.

First and Last Words. Baton Rouge: Louisiana State University Press, 1989.

The World between the Eyes. Baton Rouge: Louisiana State University Press,
1990. [Reprints 1971 edition.]

C. Baton Rouge: Louisiana State University Press, 1993.

WILLIAM HARMON

William Harmon's poems—like his conversation, his poetry classes, and his es-says—are the product of a remarkably eclectic and imaginative mind, one that not only entertains diverse topics (say, the Bhagavadgita, a cat named Zubby, and polka-dot summer pajamas) but discovers the similarity in these dissimilars and brings them together into a poetic whole. But though they are intellectual tours de force, his poems display a decorous modesty, a sharp sense of humor about their speaker and his unusual worldview, and a disarming emotional directness. And, especially compared with the verbal pell-mell of his early books, his more recent work offers the pleasures of traditional form.

Harmon's abilities have been evident from an early age. He was born in Concord, North Carolina, in 1938, but left before finishing high school to attend the University of Chicago, from which he graduated when only twenty. After service in the navy in Vietnam, he earned his Ph.D. and came to teach at the University of North Carolina at Chapel Hill, where he rose from instructor to professor in only seven years, and where he still teaches, as James G. Hanes Professor of English.

His professional accomplishments are as varied as his interests and experience. Besides five books of poetry, the first of which (*Treasury Holiday*) won the Lamont Prize in 1970, he has published a critical study of Ezra Pound; a literary magazine parody, *Uneeda Review*, with colleague Louis D. Rubin, Jr.; new editions of the standard reference work *A Handbook to Literature*; an anthology, *The Oxford Book of American Light Verse*; and two recent collections, *The Concise Columbia Book of Poetry* and *The Top 500 Poems*, which gather the most-anthologized poems of all time, with Harmon's own deft commentary.

Legion: Civic Choruses. Middletown, Conn.: Wesleyan University Press, 1973.

The Intussusception of Miss Mary America. Santa Cruz, Calif.: Kayak Books, 1976.

One Long Poem. Baton Rouge: Louisiana State University Press, 1982.

Mutatis Mutandis: 27 Invoices. Middletown, Conn.: Wesleyan University Press, 1985.

SUSAN LUDVIGSON

"And love," writes Susan Ludvigson, in the first of her poems selected for this book, "Imagine it." That's just what she's been doing for six books now: imagining love, that most difficult of subjects to write about without turning sentimental or cynical. Some of her most potent poems are about "love gone," as she succinctly calls it, relationships that have soured or darkened or fallen apart. But she can also write sensuous celebratory poems about "the escape into flesh" of innocent lovers, as in the passionate terza rima of "Paris Aubade."

Of course, like any accomplished poet, Ludvigson can write about other things: her Wisconsin past, her wide-ranging travel and reading, and especially art. Many of her books feature at least one long sequence—impossible to excerpt for this anthology—based on a work of art or an artist: the photographs of *Wisconsin Death Trip*, Scandinavian paintings from the turn of the century, or "The Life of Camille Claudel, Sculptor." The latter, a nineteen-part poem, is a powerful lyric biography detailing Claudel's involvement with "the master, Rodin," and its descent from early rapture ("a woman whose joy has found / its voice in marble") to later despair, from love to bitter hatred: "Everything you've said has turned to salt, / it penetrates my skin, / so that I work all day with a sense / that my whole body's burning."

Susan Ludvigson was born in Rice Lake, Wisconsin, in 1942, and has earned degrees from the University of Wisconsin at River Falls and the University of North Carolina at Charlotte. She moved to Charlotte in the early 1970s (the Queen City, like many North Carolina towns large and small, has a vigorous poetry scene: the statewide renaissance has solid local roots) and has been in the area ever since, when not living abroad on a Fulbright or Rockefeller fellowship or giving readings in France or Yugoslavia or Crete. She is now professor of English and poet in residence at Winthrop College in Rock Hill, South Carolina.

Step Carefully in Night Grass. Winston-Salem, N.C.: John F. Blair, 1974. [as Susan L. Bartels]

Northern Lights. Baton Rouge: Louisiana State University Press, 1981.

The Swimmer. Baton Rouge: Louisiana State University Press, 1984.

The Beautiful Noon of No Shadow. Baton Rouge: Louisiana State University
Press, 1986.

To Find the Gold. Baton Rouge: Louisiana State University Press, 1990.

Everything Winged Must Be Dreaming. Baton Rouge: Louisiana State University
Press, 1993.

MICHAEL McFEE

Michael McFee was born in Asheville, North Carolina, in 1954 and raised south of
town in Arden, where he attended Buncombe County schools. He took his B.A.
and M.A. degrees from the University of North Carolina at Chapel Hill and has
lived in Durham since 1979, working at a variety of jobs—editor, librarian, book
reviewer, and teacher. He has taught creative writing at the University of North
Carolina at Greensboro, Cornell University, Lawrence University, and (currently)
his alma mater.

Like Fred Chappell, Robert Morgan, and Jonathan Williams—other poets from
western North Carolina—McFee finds much material in his native mountains. His
first book, *Plain Air*, was (at least in part) a study of the landscape of the moun-
tains; his second, *Vanishing Acts*, had a series of "imaginary elegies" based on
various characters from his mountain upbringing; and his third, *Sad Girl Sitting
on a Running Board*, explored the mystery of the life of a representative mountain
woman of this century. But, also like his fellow mountain poets, McFee writes
other kinds of poems as well: his latest book, *To See*, is a series of poems based on
the photographs of Elizabeth Matheson, printed on facing pages.

For over a decade, McFee has devoted much energy to book reviewing—for
newspapers and magazines (chiefly *The Spectator* in Raleigh), for radio (chiefly
WUNC-FM in Chapel Hill), and for critical journals. His focus has been the
writers of the Triangle area and the state who have led the contemporary literary
revival; his aim has been to pay them the kind of careful attention they deserve but
don't always get, either at home or away. This book is another part of that effort.

Plain Air. Gainesville: University Presses of Florida, 1983.

Vanishing Acts. Frankfort, Ky.: Gnomon Press, 1989.

Sad Girl Sitting on a Running Board. Frankfort, Ky.: Gnomon Press, 1991.

To See. Rocky Mount: North Carolina Wesleyan College Press, 1991.

HEATHER ROSS MILLER

Heather Ross Miller began her career as a fiction writer. From 1964 through 1976,
she published four well-received novels and a collection called *A Spiritual Divorce
and Other Stories.* And though she studied poetry with Randall Jarrell at the

University of North Carolina at Greensboro and published several books of poems in the late 1960s and early 1970s, only in recent years has her vigorous poetry truly come into its own.

Like the other fiction-writing poets in this collection—Fred Chappell, Robert Morgan, and Reynolds Price—Heather Ross Miller handles fictional elements such as character and dramatic scene and narrative particularly well. But what really distinguishes her poetry is its voice: edgy, funny, audacious, willing to engage the difficult realities of family, history, gender, myth, and the physical world. "I am in danger," she realizes; "years go by and good things don't happen." And yet, despite the danger and the disappointments and "The Dying Off of Your Menfolks, Uncles and Fathers, Brothers, Husbands, and Sons," her poems are not bitter or self-pitying: they are spoken by one who survives, and prevails, and achieves "the peace of a tough woman." Tears may "fall in," when she's making bread and poems, "teasing the helpless dough," but still she can conclude: "Stop it, brothers. / I've got life up to the elbow."

Heather Ross Miller was born in 1939 in Albemarle, North Carolina, part of the Ross "writing family" of nearby Badin—father Fred, uncle James, aunt Eleanor. After graduating from UNC-Greensboro, she lived for years in Singletary Lake State Park with her children and husband, who was chief forester of the area. She is now professor of English at Washington and Lee University in Lexington, Virginia.

Horse Horse Tyger Tyger. Charlotte, N.C.: Red Clay Books, 1973.

Hard Evidence. Columbia: University of Missouri Press, 1990.

Friends and Assassins. Columbia: University of Missouri Press, 1993.

ROBERT MORGAN

"Make something happen in every line." That's how Robert Morgan once described the principle behind his poems, which are remarkable for their power of concentration, especially their imagistic compression. No poet wields keener metaphors than Morgan: even a brief poem like "Lightning Bug," with only fifteen octosyllabic lines, contains at least a dozen similes and metaphors, a feat of compression and invention that takes the poem's familiar Southern subject and makes it wholly new.

Morgan likes to find poems in unlikely places—in an automobile odometer, for example, or a peculiar old carpenter's term. But he also writes wonderfully vivid poems about familiar matters, in particular the geography and history of his native western North Carolina mountains, which he has been writing about for a quarter of a century—in nine books of poems, in several collections of short stories, and in a novel. He has also paid attention to overlooked forms: the present selection includes a terza rima sonnet ("Earache"), a pantoum ("Audubon's Flute"), and a chant royal ("Chant Royal"), one of the most complex French verse forms.

Robert Morgan was born in 1944 in Hendersonville, North Carolina, and grew up on the family farm in Zirconia, south of town. He began college at North Carolina State University, as a math major; but a creative writing course with Guy Owen changed his direction. He graduated from the University of North Carolina at Chapel Hill (B.A., 1965) and the University of North Carolina at Greensboro (M.F.A., 1968) and since 1971 has taught at Cornell University, where he is now Kappa Alpha Professor of English. He has received many honors, including the Eunice Tietjens Prize from *Poetry* magazine, a Guggenheim and four NEA fellowships, and the North Carolina Award for Literature.

Land Diving. Baton Rouge: Louisiana State University Press, 1976.

Trunk & Thicket. Fort Collins, Colo.: L'Epervier Press, 1978.

Groundwork. Frankfort, Ky.: Gnomon Press, 1979.

At the Edge of the Orchard Country. Middletown, Conn.: Wesleyan University Press, 1987.

Sigodlin. Middletown, Conn.: Wesleyan University Press, 1990.

Green River: New and Selected Poems. Middletown, Conn.: Wesleyan University Press, 1991.

REYNOLDS PRICE

Though Reynolds Price is one of North Carolina's best-known writers, it is probably not for his poetry. From his dazzling debut with *A Long and Happy Life* in 1962 to the more recent critical triumph of *Kate Vaiden* in 1986, he has been most celebrated for his novels. But Price has conquered many genres: he has also published collections of short stories, essays, plays, and translations from the Bible, as well as a memoir—all written in a rich, alert, unique style.

His poems address—in more compressed and personal fashion—concerns common to all his work. "Both prose and verse," Price has said, "share a conviction that nine-tenths of human experience—daily life—is intelligible to patient scrutiny and communicable in a language whose intense concerns are economy, verisimilitude, and an unflagging ear for the silent music of human action. Even the briefest personal lyrics are narrative in their assumptions and procedures—convinced of the visible continuity of human gesture and of the power inherent in attentive portrayals of such gestures: the power to guess, at least, at realities which lie invisibly but overwhelmingly behind the visible and tangible." In recent years, "daily life" for Price has meant dealing with the spinal cancer that left him in a wheelchair in 1984: each of his last two books has featured a long poetic journal confronting that "physical devastation" and its consequences.

Reynolds Price was born in Macon, North Carolina, in 1933, and raised and educated in various small towns. He graduated from Duke University and Merton College, Oxford, where he was a Rhodes Scholar; he returned to Duke in 1958 and began the teaching career he still continues as James B. Duke Professor of English. His fiction has won numerous awards, and his poetry has won the Levinson, Blumenthal, and Tietjens prizes from *Poetry*.

Vital Provisions. New York: Atheneum, 1982.
The Laws of Ice. New York: Atheneum, 1986.
The Use of Fire. New York: Atheneum, 1990.

JAMES SEAY

If any Southern state rivals North Carolina for producing fine contemporary writers, it's probably Mississippi: once a word-lavish Wolfe or Faulkner seeds the soil, the subsequent harvests can be considerable. As in North Carolina, in Mississippi the fiction writers—such as Eudora Welty, Elizabeth Spencer, and Barry Hannah—may be more famous, but the state's contemporary poets (including Jack Butler, Turner Cassity, and T. R. Hummer) are also worthy of attention.

One of those poets is James Seay, whom both states can claim. He was born in Panola County, Mississippi, in 1939 and took a degree from the University of Mississippi in 1964; but since 1974, he has taught at the University of North Carolina at Chapel Hill, where he is now professor of English and director of the Creative Writing Program. He has also taught at Vanderbilt University, the University of Alabama, and the Virginia Military Institute.

That Seay has roots in many Southern states is more than just a biographical matter. Like James Applewhite's, his poetry is obsessed with place, drawn to the haunted characters and stories that are part of the regional landscape, from Elvis in Memphis to a beach house on the Outer Banks, from the Blue Ridge Mountains to a swamp river in the Deep South. "More and more," as he writes in the last lines of his latest book, "often all I remember / is this or that landscape we passed through on our way somewhere." That way is often a dark one, riddled with bittersweet realities and memories; but with Seay it's always edged with the light of humor and hope, as when he and his wife see "The noseless three-fingered politician / on local TV who was burned in the war: / when he jumped ex tempore / into a four-point speech with a finger for each point, / there wasn't a doubt about how to face the moment together."

Water Tables. Middletown, Conn.: Wesleyan University Press, 1974.

The Light As They Found It. New York: William Morrow, 1990.

JONATHAN WILLIAMS

"I am," Jonathan Williams once said, "a poet, publisher, essayist, hiker, populist, elitist, and sorehead." "He is," Guy Davenport elaborated, "what used to be called an enthusiast, and his array of enthusiasm would take a committee of lesser souls to see." Since his days at Black Mountain College, where, in the early 1950s, he began Jargon Press by publishing poets like Charles Olson and Robert Creeley, Williams has passionately cultivated what he calls "the gospel of beauty," "all that is singular and eccentric." He is a visionary in pursuit of other visionaries, "the strays and mavericks, the generous, the non-adventitious; i.e., those afflicted with both vision and craft."

But Williams's wide-ranging, enthusiastic, sometimes cranky character should not obscure a basic fact: he is, as his self-description makes clear, first and foremost a *poet*, one who has been writing a crisp, inimitable idiom for four decades now. Like one of his favorite mavericks, Muhammad Ali, Williams's poems float like a butterfly and sting like a bee: they are capable of gorgeous romantic phrasing, but his pacing and craft and sharp sense of humor keep the poet and his readers honest. Williams also excels at found poems, fragments discovered on the road and transformed (by their presentation on the page and often hyperextended titles) into peculiarly sublime art.

Jonathan Williams was born in Asheville, North Carolina, in 1929 and graduated from St. Albans School, Princeton University, and the Institute of Design in Chicago. But his real education came at Black Mountain, where he blossomed as poet, publisher, photographer, connoisseur of arts visual and culinary, and "curator of American iconography." He divides his time between a farm near Highlands, North Carolina, and a seventeenth-century shepherd's cottage in Dentdale, Cumbria, England. Everywhere he goes (and he goes everywhere), his Catullan motto is: "I love and I hate and that's all she wrote!"

Elite/Elate Poems: Selected Poems, 1971–1975. Highlands, N.C.: The Jargon
    Society, 1979.

Get Hot or Get Out: A Selection of Poems, 1957–1981. Metuchen, N.J.: Scarecrow
    Press, 1982.

Blues & Roots / Rue & Bluets: A Garland for the Southern Appalachians.
    Durham, N.C.: Duke University Press, 1985.

Index of Titles

. . . .

Index of First Lines

Permissions

· · · · · · · ·

BETTY ADCOCK. "Southbound" and "Walking Out," from *Walking Out*, © 1975 by Betty Adcock. "Hand Made," "One Street," "Front Porch," "Roller Rink," and "Poetry Workshop in a Maximum Security Reform School," from *Nettles*, © 1983 by Betty Adcock. "Clearing Out, 1974," "Remembering Brushing My Grandmother's Hair," "Exchange," and "Rent House," from *Beholdings*, © 1988 by Betty Adcock. Reprinted by permission of the author and Louisiana State University Press.

A. R. AMMONS. "Uppermost," "Double Exposure," "Ballad," "Certainty," and "80-Proof," from *Diversifications*, © 1975 by A. R. Ammons. "Strolls," "Rapids," "Easter Morning," "Night Finding," "Parting," and "Wiring," from *A Coast of Trees*, © 1981 by A. R. Ammons. "I Went Back" and "The Role of Society in the Artist," from *Worldly Hopes*, © 1982 by A. R. Ammons. "Trigger," "Dusk Water," "Windy Morning with a Little Sleet," and "Singling & Doubling Together," from *Lake Effect Country*, © 1983 by A. R. Ammons. "Late Look," from *The Really Short Poems of A. R. Ammons*, © 1990 by A. R. Ammons. Reprinted by permission of W. W. Norton & Company, Inc.

MAYA ANGELOU. "Country Lover," "Momma Welfare Roll," and "The Memory," from *And Still I Rise*, © 1978 by Maya Angelou. "A Good Woman Feeling Bad," "Contemporary Announcement," and "Amoebaean for Daddy," from *Shaker, Why Don't You Sing?*, © 1983 by Maya Angelou. "Why Are They Happy People?" and "Preacher, Don't Send Me," from *I Shall Not Be Moved*, © 1990 by Maya Angelou. Reprinted by permission of Random House, Inc.

JAMES APPLEWHITE. "A Vigil," from *Statues of the Grass*, © 1975 by James Applewhite. Reprinted by permission of the author and the University of Georgia Press. "Some Words for Fall," "Tobacco Men," and "White Lake," from *Following Gravity*, © 1980 by James Applewhite. Reprinted by permission of the author and the University Press of Virginia. "Barbecue Service," "Collards," "Greene County Pastoral," "A Leaf of Tobacco," "Earth Lust," and "Southern Voices," from *Ode to the Chinaberry Tree and Other Poems*, © 1986 by James Applewhite; "Summer Revival" and "The Descent," from *Lessons in Soaring*, © 1989 by James Applewhite; "News of Pearl Harbor," "My Cousin Sue's Broad View," and "The Cemetery next to Contentnea," from *A History of the River*, © 1993 by James Applewhite. Reprinted by permission of the author and Louisiana State University Press.

GERALD BARRAX. "Something I Know about Her," "Body Food," and "Another Fellow," from *An Audience of One*, © 1980 by Gerald Barrax. Reprinted by permission of the author and the University of Georgia Press. "Who Needs No Introduction," "Spirituals, Gospels," "One More Word," "Two Figures on Canvas," "Portraits," and "Liberation," from *The Deaths of Animals and Lesser Gods*, © 1984 by Gerald Barrax. Reprinted by permission of the author and the University

Press of Virginia. "Domestic Tranquility," "Theology," "Strangers Like Us: Pittsburgh, Raleigh, 1945–1985," "What More?," "Haunted House," and "Adagio," from *Leaning Against the Sun*, © 1992 by Gerald Barrax. Reprinted by permission of the author and the University of Arkansas Press.

KATHRYN STRIPLING BYER. "Wide Open, These Gates," "Drought," "My Beautiful Grandmother," "Angels," and "Kitchen Sink," from *The Girl in the Midst of the Harvest*, © 1986 by Kathryn Stripling Byer. Reprinted by permission of the author and Texas Tech University Press. "Wildwood Flower," "All Hallows Eve," "Lost Soul," "Lullaby," "Thaw," "Quilt," "Lineage," "Diamonds," and "Easter," from *Wildwood Flower*, © 1992 by Kathryn Stripling Byer. Reprinted by permission of the author and Louisiana State University Press.

FRED CHAPPELL. "My Grandfather Gets Doused," from *River*, © 1975 by Fred Chappell. "Rimbaud Fire Letter to Jim Applewhite," from *Bloodfire*, © 1978 by Fred Chappell. "My Mother Shoots the Breeze," from *Wind Mountain*, © 1979 by Fred Chappell. "My Father Washes His Hands," from *Earthsleep*, © 1980 by Fred Chappell. "A Prayer for the Mountains," "The Story," "Abandoned Schoolhouse on Long Branch," and "Narcissus and Echo," from *Source*, © 1985 by Fred Chappell. "Teller," from *First and Last Words*, © 1989 by Fred Chappell. "Daisy," "First Novel," "Upon a Confessional Poet," "Literary Critic," "Another," "Another," "Televangelist," "El Perfecto," and "Apology," from *C*, © 1993 by Fred Chappell. Reprinted by permission of the author and Louisiana State University Press.

WILLIAM HARMON. "Mothsong," "The House," "Redounding," "Totem-Motet," "Zubby Sutra," "The Lilies of the Field Know Which Side Their Bread Is Buttered On," "Where Scars Come From," and "There," from *One Long Poem*, © 1982 by William Harmon. Reprinted by permission of the author and Louisiana State University Press. "The Missionary Position," "A Masque of Resignation," "Sunday Morning," and "He-Who-May-Say," from *Mutatis Mutandis: 27 Invoices*, © 1985 by William Harmon. Reprinted by permission of the author and the University Press of New England (for Wesleyan University Press).

SUSAN LUDVIGSON. "In the Beginning," "Jeanne d'Arc," "Mary," and "The Widow," from *Northern Lights*, © 1981 by Susan Ludvigson. "Some Notes on Courage" and "Man Arrested in Hacking Death Tells Police He Mistook Mother-in-Law for Raccoon," from *The Swimmer*, © 1984 by Susan Ludvigson. "The Man Who Loves Coal," "Paris Aubade," and "New Physics," from *To Find the Gold*, © 1990 by Susan Ludvigson. "Poem to the Ideal Reader" and "Lasting," from *Everything Winged Must Be Dreaming*, © 1993 by Susan Ludvigson. Reprinted by permission of the author and Louisiana State University Press.

MICHAEL McFEE. "Directions," from *Plain Air*, © 1983 by Michael McFee. Reprinted by permission of the author and the University Press of Florida. "First Radio," "Bach, Beethoven, Brahms, Mendelssohn, Mozart, Schubert, and Schumann," "Shooting Baskets at Dusk," "Cold Quilt," "Uncle Homer Meets Carl Sandburg," and "Backwards through the Baptist Hymnal," from *Vanishing Acts*, © 1989 by